Sowing the Seeds of Change:

The Organizers Handbook

Table of Contents

For the generations who came before us,

and planted seeds of justice -- we are grateful.

For the generations to come,

may these tools foster growth

for the seeds of justice, we plant today -- we are hopeful.

Intro

"We the people of the United States, in order to form a more perfect Union, establish Justice, insure domestic Tranquility, provide for the common defense, promote the general Welfare, and secure the Blessings of Liberty to ourselves and our Posterity, do ordain and establish this Constitution for the United States of America."

In the 4th Grade, I read the United States Constitution. I was astounded by the delicate balance of how a document could ensure the majority's right to make a decision. On the other hand, The Constitution also protects the right of the minority to have their voices heard. The concept of how we could all work together through differences to create a greater good. Everyone is entitled to their opinion and to have their thoughts heard. This ignited a passion for governmental structures and creating broad community change. The kind of change that happens inside and outside of traditional systems.

The way to create this change is by organizing. While organizing takes many shapes, it comes down to bringing people together around a common goal. My hope in writing this book is that it can be a guide that will enable you to create the kind of change in your community you want to see. This change may be protecting your community from toxic runoff. Or perhaps the change you want is to ensure more access to healthcare. It could be as simple as getting a new stoplight at an intersection. Or your change may be complex, like creating a more open community. Regardless of the kind of change you want, organizing is the tool that will help you make it happen. This book will offer you the knowledge of how to make it happen no matter your level of experience. I hope that this handbook will empower citizens to create a better world.

At the end of the day, politics is not the glamorous back and forth banter of The West Wing, VEEP, or House of Cards. The actual creation of change happens at the grassroots. The things that change the world are conversations at kitchen tables, knocking on doors, and sharing powerful ideas. I have seen

moms, students, people with disabilities, and everyday citizens

take on powerful forces. I have seen a group of family farmers

take on and beat a multinational corporation. I've seen kids with

disabilities take on a billionaire Governor. I've seen how one

person's good deeds can change the world. This book is a guide

to help you create that kind of change in any community for any

cause.

I've broken this book down into several major sections.

The Basics walks you through simple tools to help you

understand the main parts of organizing. We need to build a

solid foundation from which we can grow. Much of this work is

about resilience. Can you knock on another door, make another

call, keep going when it seems like there is no hope. My former

boss, Senator Ken Haar, talked about how he was like a shark

and had to keep swimming. The man's persistence to keep

moving forward to the next thing showed how this could make a

difference.

"One of the problems of organizing in the North, in the rich countries, is that people tend to think - even the activists - that instant gratification is required. You constantly hear: 'Look, I went to a demonstration, and we didn't stop the war so what's the use of doing it again?'"

Noam Chomsky

Second, we will discuss the tools to make these things happen. Having concrete tools that can help you leverage tremendous change. This is what will help you to take your local movement and expand exponentially. Without the right tools you will permanently be scrapping just to keep things moving.

Third, we will talk about the characteristics of different types of communities. Community organizing requires bringing together tremendously disparate groups of people. I find myself building bridges between hard-core partisans on both sides of the aisle. The key is finding themes and issues that are core to who they are. Power comes by discovering themes and issues that can bring people together. You need to understand a community and respect their interests to do so.

Last, we will discuss stories about ethics, drive, and what inspires us to create change. It matters that you remember why you are doing what you are doing. Without a solid ethical compass that remains grounded, you will lose your way. This requires a deep level of focus and intentionality. The best way to do this is to consult other perspectives and focus on those stories that ground your values.

I felt compelled to write this book because I was a young organizer who lived in a rural area. With most of the state's seasoned operatives 100+ miles away, it was difficult to find quality mentors. When I did get to work with seasoned operatives, I maximized those learning opportunities. This led me to lots of non-traditional sources.

I hope this guidebook can provide you with the essential tools to create change. It shouldn't matter where you live, who you know, or what resources you have. Everyone should have access to the tools required to create this kind of change.

This passion for our democratic process started me off on a trajectory early. In Middle School, I had my first internship for a State Senator and Secretary of State. While it was only data entry, it's led to some incredible experiences. Experiences like arguing with then-Vice President Biden about pushing harder for action on rural broadband. To pass innovative bipartisan legislation to help ensure more election accessibility. Or starting a solar company to develop renewable energy in the private market when policy leaders wouldn't take action. I hope that this book can help you better understand how to create that change. That this change will be morally guided, encourage broader participation, and grow a robust democracy.

Basics

Organizing at its core is about connecting with people. To lead a community, you have to start by listening and understanding. Many people try to volunteer to offer advice on policy or strategy. The truth is that most people are not actually ready to enter at that high of a level. They need to start by listening, understanding, and digging in, and doing the basics. The most seasoned of quality operatives know they always need to get back to basics. There is nothing more powerful than picking up a phone, a clipboard, or fliers to hand out. Because as you talk with people, you understand what people want. You can also understand the arguments against you and how to address those concerns.

When first meeting with a person, I will ask, "What drives you? Why are you here?" I want to hear their story. Hearing their story helps to develop a genuine connection. This is your path to understanding what drives them.

As well as hearing stories, it's also important to share your story. Sharing your story establishes credibility and opens the

door for a deeper connection. I have several key stories that I
tend toward. However, the most powerful story is the story of
my sister's death from suicide (which you will read more about
later). It's not an easy story to tell. If I'm feeling very open, it
involves talking about mental health issues. Some days I just
don't feel up to offering that, so I keep it brief. When I take the
deep dive, I find the connections are astounding. This has led me
to unexpected friendships and even relationships. All because of
the power of that vulnerability.

Activist/ List Building

After building relationships, your next goal is gathering people together. You need to collect contacts and target who to talk to first. You need to get those volunteers organized to do direct outreach. Finding good ways to do this is difficult but vital to ensure the community change that you want to see. The better you organize and prioritize your contacts, the more effective you will be. If your operating on a limited budget, this is particularly important.

One of my best friends and frequent collaborators is Graham Christensen. When we started working together, Graham did an excellent job collecting contacts in notebooks. This is a more old-school skill but so important. His ability to connect with people is impressive, to say the least. These natural connections are so valuable. It takes time, practice, and a bit of natural ability to build these types of relationships. But they are so valuable! Especially if you log this information into a common spot like Google Contacts.

Using Google Contacts worked for him for a long time. But when we started to build a larger entity, we needed a more advanced tool. I twisted Graham's arm to get a quality database. This next step was critical to take things to the next level and continue to expand. This shift to our database Nationbuilder has amplified our work. It multiplied the number of people we could contact and improved our ability to track and organize those folks. So let's chat a bit about how to create your own lists and databases.

Personal Lists

Whatever kind of change you are creating, you need to get to that critical mass. I tend to work for causes that upset very well-financed entities. This tends to create an uphill battle. Except I have one thing that they don't. I have dedicated, hardworking, passionate individuals. Working together with this team of volunteers creates an ability to create tremendous changes.

The best place to find those individuals is with people you know. Because if those close to you don't believe in you, then who will? That means every new project, the first people I work with are my friends, family, neighbors, and community members. Often, I know who may be likely to care about a cause and will call, text, email, etc. them first. Even if this group of people isn't interested, they may know someone who would be interested.

Sympathetic Organizations

Once you contact the people you know, you need to start looking for organizations to engage. Hopefully, there isn't another group doing exactly what you are doing. If so, there is no reason to reinvent the wheel; reconsider the usefulness of your group. But begin looking at organizations with similar missions (i.e., care about Medicaid talk to Nebraska Appleseed). Then you can figure out how you can help or partner on their pre-existing efforts or projects.

These organizations are always trying to do more than they should be able to do on limited resources. So if you can find ways to plug into their work or make it easy for them to take action, that makes a huge difference. This may be easy talking points, pre-made graphics, or creating a template press release. I've worked with many causes where these simple techniques can significantly boost your efforts. Even if you can't find direct overlap, it's good to let folks working in similar areas know what is going on. Frequently, organizations working on similar causes waste resources by failing to coordinate.

Outreach

After you have a base assembled, you can begin reaching out further. This is the point to begin large social media, news, and event outreach. This is where you start to expand and get your message out there. The larger membership from previous steps will provide the needed legitimacy for your efforts.

Sign Up Sheets

When collecting information, there are few tools as powerful as sign-up sheets. The information you may need will vary upon your cause, but here are some key factors to keep in mind:

- ☐ First Name, Last Name, Address, Phone Number, Email, Occupation, Willingness to Volunteer, Willing to Donate
- ☐ Some other factors to also consider
- ☐ Twitter Handle, Age, Political Districts, How Contacted Them
- ☐ Always Have a Clipboard

That said, it is so pivotal always to have a clipboard, Moleskine notebook, or at least your phone notes. This is a lesson that every intern and first-time organizer will learn quickly. Sign-in sheets/clipboards turn one action into an ongoing relationship to change the world. Along with the clipboard, have pens, and a positive attitude. I've seen many interns, volunteers, or staff do nothing sitting at tables for events when they should be reaching out to chat with the folks who pass by. If you aren't excited about changing the world, how will they be?

If you don't have a clipboard, get on your smartphone and add it to your contacts or whatever digital notes program you use. You never know when this will come into play. I've made key connections in some surprising places like casual social events, bars, airports, and one time even in a respite room at a hospital.

Organize Info

Once you have the information, you need to organize it in a way that works for you. If you have a good database (i.e. Nationbuilder, NGP, Salsa, etc.), it's easy to organize that information. (We will discuss using these database tools later and which ones will likely make sense for you and your purpose.) If you don't have access to one of these great resources, then it gets more complicated.

Once you grow past a few hundred members, getting some sort of database service is key. But luckily, there are lots of great tools you can use to scale up quickly. The first place to start is probably an Excel spreadsheet for a smaller organization. You can also look to free tools like Google's Sheets that now allows you to create a quick free app with the push of a few buttons. We had a lean volunteer team with no database when I was working on a state party chair race. So, we used a Google Sign Up Form and Google Sheets to add other contacts. It allowed us to have a significant quick mobilization and tracking information to quickly follow a lot of votes. Google Sheets also adds the ability to have all of your data live updated so that everyone can see it.

Transforming Information to Activation

When you have this information gathered, you need to find the best ways to use that information. There are several typical ways to activate your members:

- Email lists are the most typical, easy way to activate members

- Call Time is the best way to get folks started, although more labor-intensive

- Social media posts are the easiest way to reach a whole lot of people... If only more of them would take action

- Which method you choose depends on your goal.

I find it funny how true this can be. When I transitioned The Arc of Nebraska over to using email blasts, I faced some resistance. I found a few older members frustrated they weren't getting much physical mail. Then I talked to them about the cost benefits, and they agreed it was important. Now they are some of the people who respond the most to emails. We will dive more into this in later chapters, but I highly recommend using a hybrid approach. Combining these methods creates synergy to produce more than any individual tool.

These tools can develop great relationships with many people you've never even met. Frequently, I find people who feel like they know me because I send them email and text updates. While I work to get to know as many as I can, I cannot ensure I can remember everyone. But this is a good problem to have. It means that you are connecting and mobilizing a lot of people.

Email

Email is best for some sort of call to action. (We will later discuss the pieces of a high-caliber call to action.) It's also a solid reminder as people are forgetful and need to be reminded many times. Email is also suitable for any event that isn't open to the public.

Email Tips

Consider who the email is coming from if you have a trusted person that can build a relationship. Suppose it's a fundraising director that may make for a better financial ask. Then think about who you want to target with the email. For instance, having a polarized endorsement can engage a party base for a moderate candidate.

When not using a software program, make sure to BCC your list to protect your members' privacy. This also is a good practice to mitigate a Reply All nightmare that can be downright annoying. I've seen too many times that members' emails have been made vulnerable by an improperly used CC. This can leave your contacts vulnerable to the complete list and anywhere they forward the email.

The times to use a CC will be if you want to make sure they see it. For instance, to share a document with a group. It can also be helpful to create accountability. I tell people to CC me when they talk to DHHS because then the department knows I'm paying attention. This can elicit a quicker response because the department knows I will follow up.

As you write your text, keep text easy, short, and straightforward. The more complex that information is, the more likely people will ignore it or miss part of your messaging. People are busy and get lots of emails. So the more straightforward, the more likely people are to take action.

In this short email, you can use hyperlinks for a couple of purposes. First, hyperlinks can help you to add more depth. As you try to keep your email simple, there will always be some people who will want more detail. Second, a hyperlink can help direct people to actions on your website. This will help you to collect more info and better track who is taking action.

(See the image below for a sample of a quality blast email)

Calls

Phone calls should be a core part of any outreach plan. While calls take more time, they are also more likely to lead to action. A higher level of connection inspires more accountability. This increases the likelihood of a reply and action. Don't get discouraged by a bad first phone call because you are building relationships for the future. If you keep calling more, you may get a better reaction after those first few conversations.

Tips on Calls

Write a painfully simple script. I can't reiterate enough how important it is to keep things brief. The majority of people are far too busy, and longer emails rarely produce a large volume of actions. With any format, you are required by some law to identify yourself. Plus, it's always good to make it very clear who you are and have quality identifiers.

It also matters when you call. You may have difficulty getting good contacts. For instance, calling at 3 pm on a weekday afternoon, you may only get retirees. This can be great if you use a list of only people who are over 65. This helps you have a high contact rate in a time that might be difficult to reach other people. This can also be a barrier if you are calling in Nebraska during a Husker game.

If you have someone with a personal connection, use it. I recommend that candidates the best place to start calling is their own contacts. I recommend leveraging a candidate's phone to sync their contacts into a good call list. Lastly, always have a clear Hard Ask to get exactly what you want an individual to do (ex. Please vote for X). Once you ask that question, you need to stay quiet because whoever talks next loses.

Social Media Posts

Social Media posts are easy, quick, and can spread like wildfire. They can also be a small piece of junk in a few people's news feeds. Being able to post something to Facebook does not make you a "social media expert." However, we will talk later about techniques to start punching up your social media game.

Hints for Social Media

Consider a Social media management program like Hootsuite. Using Hootsuite to schedule your posts will cut down your work hours spent on social media. It will also help you with ensuring more consistent posts by scheduling posts. Consider the timing of your post. Shoot out emails to your staff/board to like/share the post. Use links properly. Add a graphic.

- Remember, this is just the beginning.
- As you go on, continue to use these practices to grow your membership
- Learn from what you do
- Improve as time continues

Guide to Phonebanks and Canvasses

Phone banking and Canvassing is the most fundamental part of community organizing. I run a quick test on all new candidates. I ask them to pick up their phone right now and call their best friend. If they can't ask their best friend for their support, volunteer, and donate, they are not ready to be a candidate. Because they will be making thousands of calls. These calls are to ask strangers for money, volunteer, or support, which are very heavy things to have someone entrust you with. So, you need to work to build a relationship that will build support. You also need to consider the most effective use of your time. You will be calling thousands of people, so you can only spend a limited amount of time with each person. Make sure it's the right people.

Reasons to Canvass

Canvassing offers many benefits. In-person, interactions are more personal and more effective. This means that you will have to make fewer attempts to get a good vote. On the

32

downside, it requires more people and can be more challenging. Which means it can be harder to retain volunteers.

I've seen canvassing build some fantastic relationships. When you come to someone's door, they are so much more likely to remember you. I remember one time I was knocking on doors in a small town in central Nebraska. I knocked on a gentleman's door who seemed very skeptical. As we kept talking, he changed his tune and even became a volunteer. This one volunteer then knocked on hundreds of doors. This is how one good canvassing connection can make a huge difference.

Reasons to Phonebank

Phone banks are less resource-intensive. This means that you attempt more contacts. Calling is also easier to keep volunteers and ensure they stay motivated. The downsides are that it's less personal, less effective, and there is a lower chance of contact.

But again, it's amazing how you can make and grow those connections. Again in Central Nebraska, I called a new volunteer who became a force. With a bit of support and taking some time to build a relationship, the return was exceptional. She called for us almost 40 hours a week as a volunteer! While that is a rare occurrence, it's amazing how those things can happen with a bit of a connection.

What about Both?

The most effective is a good combination of both calls and canvassing. Leverage each tool depending upon your purpose. For instance, start with phone banking to recruit your volunteers. This will be a more effective use of your time. You will also want to start volunteers as phone bankers. Beginning people as phone bankers allows them to get a feel for this kind of direct contact in a group. This makes it easier to build confidence, practice, and have fun. If you try to toss volunteers straight into canvassing, I often find that they may decide not to come back.

One time I took a new canvasser out to knock on some doors, and we went through a couple with him. He seemed to do a great job, so I split up our packet to get more doors in. I told him to meet me back there in an hour. When I came back, he wasn't there. So, I waited a while, and he still didn't come back. So, I gave him a call, and still no response. I started to get worried and started to drive around the turf.

Eventually, I found him standing in front of a door talking to a shirtless guy with a big beer belly and a ponytail. This voter had trapped the first-time canvasser in a 40-minute conversation. The voter was belligerent and harassing as he pushed conspiracy theories on us. I tried to talk to him for another ten minutes and finally said we needed to go. As we left, he continued to follow us down his property line, yelling at us. This is an extreme example but exemplifies the kind of weird positions canvassing can put you in. While this canvasser came back, many others won't.   Whereas with a phone call, you can just hang up.

How to Start

So how do you get set up? First, you need to identify the lists of people you need to talk to. Next, identify your target location. Meaning the neighborhood if canvassing or the place you can call from if phone banking. When you get this, you can start to invite your volunteers to that location.

What to have?

For your direct contact event, be sure to have all your materials. This can include call sheets, scripts, pens, talking points, clipboards, or door hangers. It's also important to have comfort and fun items. This may include water, snacks, tablets, swag items, a whiteboard to show progress towards your goal, etc.

One of the tools that we have discussed is Calls to Action. What do we get the activists who we've collected through our phone banks, canvasses, community events, personal lists, etc., to do, exactly? How can we get them to best engage in the cause? What information do they need to be part of your greater grassroots efforts?

Basic Asks

I suggest starting with basic easy actions like calls to encourage lawmakers to take action, template letters for them to just add their name to, easy digital petitions where they just have to click a button to sign on, encourage them to write a letter to the Editor or get them to attend an event. One of my favorite examples of how this has worked for me was that over an August Recess Congressman Fortenberry was doing Town Halls across the district. We sent out an email blast encouraging volunteers to ask him about a bill we were supporting. We had volunteers at three events in a row, all asking the same questions. I was at the last one, and he said, "OK, Edison, I hear you. Let's set up a meeting so you can tell me how to help." He ended up becoming a co-sponsor of that legislation. All thanks to one email blast.

Calls to a Lawmaker

I'm a big fan of leveraging calls to a lawmaker. Calls are relatively easy but allow for a conversation. The more personal your interaction, the more powerful it will be. But with a geographically spread group of citizens, sometimes it's hard to get someone down to an office.

When you push your volunteers towards calls, make sure to provide them with a summary of the issue, bullet points of arguments, the number and name of staff to address, and the hard ask (Will you vote for Bill XX?). I also try to give them a basic introductory script. I will caution you that if you give them too much, they will read off of it, and then you will just end up with agitated staffers.

Keep in mind different offices handle constituent contact in different ways. Most offices will keep a simple tally on issues, some have detailed tracking processes, and some will pretty much ignore everything. But even if an elected official ignores everything, it's still important to have calls to them. That makes it harder for them to say things like "none of my constituents care" Then, if someone says that, you can let people know they've gotten calls and if you have a good tracking system, how many calls.

Letters/Emails to Senators

Letter/Email campaigns are by far the most common outreach tool, thanks to the prevalence of the digital age. The downside is you lose some personalization and direct human contact with this method, but it's way easier to get a lot of emails than phone calls.

When setting these questions up, include an introduction to your issue, a reason, and the urgency. Then have a secondary piece that is a template email.

Template Emails/Letters

You obviously want to have a template that is timely and precise. Make sure that you get the essential information through as lobbyists can help to clarify the details. So, you may say, "Support Renewable Energy pass Bill XX." But hopefully, you are working with a lobbyist who can clarify that it's actually about Net Metering and ensuring rates that allow solar projects to competitively cash flow in a private market.

It's also helpful to include an Intro identifying them as constituents and members of your organization. Then they need a clear, hard ask that ensures that the staffer or elected official knows what they are talking about. It can also be helpful to add some background on an issue as that will add important context.

And most importantly, don't forget a Thank You or Follow Up
request.

Events

Another helpful tool when organizing is having an event.
This can take a lot of shapes, such as movie screenings, speaker
panels, informative meetings, protests, etc. Most of these events
all have a basic layout and similar structural needs. You need to
have someone in charge of the event who is loud, energized, and
dynamic to excite people. A location that is easily accessible and
equipment to ensure you can clearly communicate with everyone
or show them the movie or PowerPoint you are presenting.

Letters to the Editor

One tool that I've found very interesting in its
effectiveness is the Letter to the Editor. I'm sometimes amazed by
the people who will read it. For instance, in one of my Letters to
the Editors, I discussed the importance of continuing the civil

rights movement to ensure people with disabilities get what they need. Then local civil rights icon Senator Ernie Chambers told me he liked it.

I've also seen how this allows you to maximize the power of stories. Recently, we had a bill filibustered by a small group of senators who would have helped kids with disabilities. Families were furious and wanted to make sure that other citizens understood why this was so important. So, I gave them a spreadsheet of papers statewide and how to submit a Letter to the Editor. I told them how most papers are going to want something that is 250 words or less. Then I gave them some basic talking points but encouraged them to focus on their story. We had dozens of powerful stories shared, and I was amazed at how that connected to people we would have never usually reached. This created a tremendous groundswell of energy that led to many new community members connecting to us and our work.

Farm Team

There are many organizing templates to structure your group. I recommend using parts of generic models that you can customize for your community. This is one method among many that you can pieces or ideas for a structure. With my extensive work in rural communities, I like to talk about a Farm Team. The Farm Team means it is a growing operation that starts at the roots and grows into something powerful. I also think it's an apt analogy because you won't know what you have until it grows.

I developed this model with a tightly connected community experienced in working together. They had worked together on the PTA, church events, and nonprofit fundraisers. I built on these natural community networks in a way that enabled a smooth transition. This kind of structure is excellent for rural communities and those with strong pre-set networks.

Candidates Team

These are your ride-or-die people. The first group that you will probably see is the friends and family of the candidate. Keep in mind this may take all shapes. It's always interesting who will appear as those most dedicated volunteers. While most of the time it will be closer friends and family, that is not always the case. It could be the guy you had one class with, an old co-worker, or a friend of a friend. Invite everyone because it may surprise you who your most dedicated volunteer will be. Ideally, before running, you will have already prepared your base group, and they are ready to dive in. They will be prepared to knock doors, make phone calls, stuff envelopes, or whatever else it takes.

The next group of people is those who strongly believe in the candidate. These are people who identify with your values and like the direction you're heading. They believe that you will accomplish something on a critical issue or that you are the moral choice. This is why many people want to get involved with campaigns. This will inspire passionate acts like knocking doors in a blizzard or other dedicated acts.

Another reason to get involved in campaigns is a belief in the candidate as a person. They have a good gut feeling about the candidate. Or the volunteer is impressed by what the candidate says. It can also be that they believe the candidate is better than the current officeholder.

Team Roles

Farm Team Leaders

Farm team leaders, these people are the basic backbone, the very essence of the campaign. They drive everything. Great ideas and effective policies don't make a difference if you don't get the message out. The farm team leader's job is to get out and talk with individuals of the most local level.

On the other hand, they don't just take out information if they're doing their job right. The farm team leaders bring back information from the neighbors they have talked to. This information gathering helps to keep the campaign connected to

47

community needs. It ensures the issues of the community stay at the heart of your message. This will help you to transcend the noise and clearly communicate. Here are the basics of how they should do their outreach.

Canvassing Steps

Step 1

· Try to memorize and analyze the info you have on the voter

· Approach door respectfully (don't walk on the grass)

· Ring the doorbell or knock in a firm fashion

· Wait 30-45 seconds

Step 2

· If they open the door, proceed to step 3

· If they don't open the door, place the leaflet in the crack of the door

· DO NOT PLACE THE LEAFLET IN THE MAILBOX!!!

Step 3

· Greet resident in a kind fashion similar to that in script

48

· Identify yourself

· Verify that you have the correct resident

· If you do not have the correct resident see if they are available

Step 4

· Proceed with Script

· To the best of your ability, make it a conversation

· Get as far through the script as you can, respectfully

· Thank them for their time. Being a good citizen is hard work

· Leave them a leaflet

Step 5

· Record answer

· Continue to next house quickly

· Repeat from step 1

Do's and Don'ts of Canvassing

Do

· Be respectful

· Ask questions if necessary

· Knock as many doors as possible in a complete fashion

Don't

· Get into violent arguments

· Use profanity

· Do anything that would negatively reflect on the campaign

Potential Issues

· Police have an issue with you

· Voter won't let you go

· You feel unsafe

· You have any question

Social Media Watchdogs

Social Media Watchdogs can take a variety of approaches to their roles. At the core, they track key digital community discussions, report, and be ready to react. This has been a position that I've seen go all sorts of ways. Most people aren't used to dealing with social media in such a disciplined way. So it can be helpful to create a bit more structure. You can give them a template for regularly scheduled practices. Some suitable activities are checking certain pages, posting with specific tags, or a goal number of comments. Their key responsibilities are:

· Post information about the candidate/cause on other pages

· Help invite people to events

· If any "trolls" put false information, then help us to provide facts instead of fiction

· General messaging from the campaign

· Events for the campaign

· Volunteer opportunities or highlights of what volunteers have done

· Fundraising because it never hurts to ask again

Yard Sign Team

You need people to work together to ensure yard signs are strategically placed around the district. Then set a date to have a yard sign release, so it looks like a large swell of energy. Team members will help to monitor yard signs and ensure we are following the law.

Yard Sign Rules

Political signs, posters, advertisements, or notices cannot be attached, fastened, or connected, in any manner, to any of the following public areas: Curbstones, a portion of any sidewalk or street, Trees, Posts, Poles, Hydrants, Bridges, Other public structures within the limits of any street right of way.

Editorial Writers

You need folks who are willing to help write and publish letters to the Editor about the candidate. Letters are to highlight why the candidate should be our representative. Personal stories can hit emotional triggers. It can also help to get respected members of the community who will sway others' opinions. Keep in mind the better the quality of writing, the more likely it will be published.

Political engagement also requires engaging with your elected officials. One of the best opportunities for this is with public hearings. Hearings are your time to lift up issues that matter to you.

One of the benefits of hearings is that it's one of the few times an elected official is forced to listen. Assuming that they don't fall asleep in the hearing. So coming ready to knock these out of the park can be vital to whether your issues move forward or not.

Preparation

Look over the bill and find specifics that you would like to see changed. Get specific information on the hearing and purpose. If possible, get onto the agenda. If not, give courtesy calls to committee chairs or sponsoring elected officials. In particular, it is helpful to talk to the bill/motion sponsors. Also, reach out to those friendly organizations that we've discussed. And sometimes organizations that are less friendly but align with you on this issue.

Line up Testifiers

This is much like a legislative meeting, with more people and formality. When lining up, potential testifiers try to get a variety of backgrounds. Try to balance professionals with people directly impacted by the legislation. Ensure these are well-spoken individuals. Then line up as many people as possible. (Also, look at the Storytelling Chapter for more ideas on preparing speakers.) Once you get this together, take some time and practice.

Preparation

Silly little things often make a difference. I've seen Senators turned off by people who don't seem to be respectfully dressed. Or small things like having copies of your testimony can make a difference. So have information packets with your HARD ASK. And arrive early.

Testifiers

Some helpful instructions for testifiers are to address the committee respectfully. Keep to time limits as going overtakes time from everyone else. Be prepared to do Social Media Live, whether Facebook Live recording it or live-tweeting.   Distribute information packets before speaking.

Basics of Public Speaking

There are few things worse than not understanding someone who is making an effort to be heard. Don't have anything in your mouth. Next, stretch out your mouth by opening your mouth as wide as you can for 30 seconds. You will find that this will improve your volume and clarity. I also see people tend to speak too quickly or too slowly. Easy tools to control your pace are having a timer or writing reminders in your notes. I will also sometimes have a person to signal in the crowd. Of course, that requires that the speaker looks at their signal person. One time I had a candidate who would not stop talking, and I kept trying to signal him, but he didn't look over.

When speaking to a room, you need to have a whole different mindset. I find the most common issue is when people try to speak like they are having a conversation with someone next to them. Instead, you should be thinking about filling the whole room with your sound. You need to picture your sound as a physical thing and think about pushing it past the back wall. This technique will ensure everyone hears you and that your sound will fill the room as your sound bounces all around.

Many people try to speak without having it physically written down. You can do this, but everyone is better with notes. No matter how many times you speak, sometimes you will trip up or forget something. This also gives you a lot of opportunities to add in little notes or signals to yourself.

The most common things to write are: slow down, speed up, smile, hash marks to pause, reminders to look up, areas to add extra emphasis, and increase your sound near the end of a sentence, so you don't drop off.

Be Prepared for Questions

Since you never know what bit you may forget, notes are essential. Even issues I could previously regurgitate in my sleep, sometimes I've found difficult to remember at the moment. Or even simple mistakes. For instance, I once confused two bills interstate reciprocity conditions. I was thinking of a bill for doctors who served people with hearing disabilities. But the family ranch program I had in mind did not have the same reciprocity. So I had to go back and correct myself. This mix-up is why notes of important facts or numbers can be so important. You should also have a list of resources for follow-up or a handout.

Most importantly, be prepared to say "I don't know" and follow up. Or if you do mess up as I did on the interstate reciprocity issue, make sure to follow up and correct yourself.

Follow Up

Once an event ends doesn't mean that your work is finished. The follow-up is arguably even more important sometimes. So make sure to get members all the info requested.

If you want to make, a good impression, write Thank You notes or emails with some Follow Up Asks. For instance, if you had a good conversation on a tangential issue, then follow up. Send them more information, ask for a meeting to discuss that issue, or suggest policy changes.

You can also use those events to help launch more public dialogue. I encourage a quick Social Media follow-up post on the topic. I frequently find at hearings that reporters are looking for comments on their stories. Depending on the situation, it can also be helpful to look at a Letter to the Editor or Press Release. It might be hard to get the press to pick up on a story if they didn't

show up to the hearing. If you don't get a story, an alternative

route is a Letter to the Editor to ensure you have something in

the papers.

Campaign/Cause Fundraising

One essential piece of any organizing effort or campaign is to have the funds to make it happen. You need cash to get your message out, pay your staff, continue your effort, and keep the cause moving forward. I know that public perception is frequently that campaign/lobbying fundraising is evil. But I would argue that if done right, it's a tremendously ethical calling.

There are many challenges to fundraising effectively and ethically. But it's absolutely vital for your work. These funds can help broaden your reach, improve your messaging, provide research, create compelling graphics or even basics like pay for gas to get to an event. Change doesn't happen if you can't pay for mailers, signs, staff, buttons, etc.

Fundraising can also significantly increase your efficiency. Once I told a candidate that he could knock doors for 3 hours a week for the next year or throw a good fundraiser. When reaching out to large groups, your time becomes so important. One resource you will never get back is more time.

Why Do People Give to a Campaign/Cause?

There are many reasons why individuals give to campaigns or causes. Some motivations are more selfish, and some are more selfless. Either way, understanding motivations is vital to help raise more funds. Those motivations determine how you interact with donors and develop your fundraising plan.

I typically find there are one or two key issues that people will connect with a candidate. I had a volunteer who worked tirelessly because the candidate pledged to fix property taxes. Sometimes it's because you have spent time working with them and their community. It can also be helpful if they identify with you, who you are, and what you are trying to do.

Personal connections can also make a huge difference. I've found some of the best volunteers are those who know the person is asking. Maybe they've worked with you on other issues or campaigns. Sometimes it can also be helpful if they know people who work on the campaign. For instance, I've had my staff call my mom and get her to commit to a shift. Or sometimes, endless persistence can build a relationship. I've had people who have sat on prospective volunteer lists for an entire season. After dozens of calls, they end up finally taking a shift for election day. It can also be due to a less optimistic sort of incentive. One of the strongest drivers is that they dislike the other candidate.

It can also be helpful if the donor sees some potential gain. Lobbyists with specific interests are some of the most frequent donors. This can be a negative. But it can also be helpful if a company aligns with your values. For instance, a renewable energy company that supports a candidate who wants to grow wind energy.

Development Tools

Recurring Donors

Many organizations struggle with ensuring a steady monthly cash flow. The organization ends up in boom and bust cycles. This makes it difficult to plan and requires staff time to ask for another donation. Instead, you can eliminate that staff cost by asking for recurring donors. This will level out your cash flow and, if done right, ensure more total funds are donated. Even a simple $5 donation creates increased stability and the ability to plan. For instance, 50-100 donors at an average of $20 per donor may not sound large. But that can produce $1000-2000/month or $12000-24000/year for your program.

Increased Events

Many organizations, early in the development process, lack enough events throughout the year. People and organizations have different funds available at varying times in the year. For instance, winter is a slower season for many farmers. A big trend to look at is end-of-year gifts as people consider tax implications. These asks at different times will produce different types of gifts. I recommend considering new events throughout the year. This can increase your fundraising, reach, and ability to help more people.

Conference

Another critical source of income for many organizations is annual conferences or dinners. That ensures these events can be fundraisers instead of financial drains. I find many times that the most helpful thing is to decrease the overhead on large events. Other changes to consider are a new marketing plan, modified sponsorships, or a shift to a hybrid event.

Sponsorships

Rarely do individual donors power a donor program. Typically, larger organizations or corporate contributions are a crucial factor. This is an area that most organizations need to work on. Sponsorships are nice because they can provide a bigger bang for your buck than an individual donor.

Sponsorships are also a key factor in expanded partnerships. You may start asking for money, but grow your collaboration as you continue to work together. I find it's hard for these interactions not to grow in scope. For instance, a company I work with started with a donation but became a regular resource for our members. Some great examples are unions, providers, corporations, membership organizations, and large private donors. But keep your eyes open for new opportunities.

Email/Social Media Asks

Social Media Content Calendar

So once you identify potential donors, how do you get more money out of them? I'm a big fan of incorporating financial asks into the social media content calendar. Regular posts for donations help to grow a steady stream of smaller donors. Just like with other donors, you never when someone will feel called to support your cause.

Weekly Email Asks

Email programs are a great way to engage current and new low-dollar donors. Engaging people with your work will help them feel more like part of the mission every week.

Hear the Grassroots

The list collection we previously discussed can also expand your fundraising. Growing that list will help you to create good people to ask for contributions. If you then tag donors based upon issues they are interested in, you can target them with specific questions. These targeted asks will get to the heart of what drives them. For instance, if you took action on the Affordable Care Act, you probably care about other Medicaid issues. So a reasonable ask would be, "We need 2310$ this month to get 300 calls into the legislature to support Medicaid."

Database and Donor Tracking

This is key to organizational development and fundraising development. You need to know who has given, how much, when, and who else has yet to give. Having more information on donors makes it easier to target them and see patterns in gifts. So if someone always donates on Giving Tuesday, they would be a good prospect for a mailer asking for a donation.

Survey Respondents

An organizational survey is a key tool to determine future direction. With that, you need to know what people are feeling to determine where you are going. This can also help to understand why people aren't giving or if they could increase their gifts. I add in the survey the option of putting your name in because then I can use that information to have a conversation around their concerns. (i.e., Someone says, "I want us to have more outreach in small towns." We can then respond, "How are you willing to help us expand our outreach?"

Planned Giving Program

Planned giving should be a considerable part of your sustainability plan. End-of-life gifts, in particular, are likely to be larger and, if placed in an endowment, can be permanent gifts. Imagine having an endowment that covers all of your annual budget needs. Then your fundraising can just be about growth.

This could be a passionate volunteer who only had $20 per month when alive. If they buy a $100,000 life insurance policy, they could suddenly give $50,000 and leave another $50,000 for family. Expanding focus on planned giving will ensure long-term organizational stability. This can be vital to get you through challenging markets or significant financial hits.

Legislative Resolutions

A Legislative Resolution takes several forms:

- A simple congratulatory statement (i.e., Celebrating Developmental Disabilities Month, Honoring Tim Kolb's Life and Service, etc.)

- Constitutional Amendments

- Interim Studies- An opportunity to do a deep dive into a complex issue.

- This can help bring parties with different perspectives together

- help to clarify complex topics

- Educate Senators and Committee Members

- Get a large amount of information into Legislative Record

- It brings press and public attention to an issue

When an Interim Study goes well, it can create conversations around important issues. For instance, LR 540 by Senator Walz was at the start about transition services funding for people with disabilities. But it started discussions on more

72

complex issues like The Waiting List and Foster Care. These conversations served as a catalyst for several bills in varying areas. This led to expanded funding, administrative changes, and improved notice standards.

How can you be Involved?

The most obvious way to get engaged is to have an Interim Study introduced. Encouraging a Senator to look more into an issue may inspire them to do a deeper dive. Sometimes the battle is simply to get them to watch a hearing. Once they hear the information, it may spark an unexpected passion for an issue.

This does assume that it will have a hearing. Which sometimes, you need to push on Committee Chairs even to have a hearing. Many Interim Hearings may not even get that sort of dedicated focus. Sometimes even a small hearing can bring a new perspective and inspire interest in an issue.

When you can get a hearing, make sure to take part and encourage others to participate. Following the hearing, make sure you get the information presented to others who weren't there. Sometimes extraordinary hearings that reveal deep insights fail to attract a large audience. So it's up to you to get that information to the broader community. This can be by bringing it to the press, sending it to your members, or distributing it at community events. It also helps if Senators introduce legislation in response to the hearing.

That is why I pay close attention to the questions or comments that Senators bring up. These comments and questions can be valuable openings to start a dialogue. Even if that discussion is more complex, it can be an opportunity for new engagement. One bill was tangentially affected by an issue for which a Senator had a considerable passion. He took us down a rabbit hole of questions on that issue. We were on different sides of the issue, but his questions opened pathways to areas of agreement. In our follow-up meeting, we were able to move forward and educate him on other matters.

Also, remember that Senators break up topics generally based upon their committee. But sometimes, they can break beyond that perspective to engage on surprising issues. So even inviting a Senator to watch an important hearing can get them into an unexpected issue. This can broaden their perspective and increase their knowledge on a subject. One time I was even able to get the Lieutenant Governor to attend a hearing. This increased his interest in the topic and led to some administrative progress.

Tools

Top Tools for Rural Organizing

Urban-based organizers often express frustration when they are first organizing in rural communities. I've found my rural volunteers and community leaders to be some of the most reliable and dedicated.

To help you get started working in rural communities, I've put together a list of tools and methods to tap. Here's what to keep in mind as you gear up for future efforts:

Tap Key Community Members

I've mentioned the importance of key community members. These folks can be some of the most effective tools in your arsenal. Sit down with these key players early on, recruit them to your side, and keep them engaged.

Use Who You Have and Adapt Your Model

The two most used organizing models are precinct-based and community-based. Both models need volunteers with particular skill sets. It can be harder to implement these models in areas with fewer people. So consider combining methods and fill roles with staff if needed.

Internet/Social Media

One advantage of broad internet adoption is the quick ability to reach a large audience. This means your message can inundate target areas with a few strategic contacts. A few well-placed contacts with good reach can efficiently get out your message. In particular, with social media, you can open new communication pathways.

Email

A well-developed email list is powerful. With a quality list, you can get your messaging quickly to lots of people. Using email in rural communities, remember that rural broadband access can be problematic. Many people in these communities are less likely to check email as frequently. To address this, increase the time out you send email blasts. This can prevent your valued volunteers from missing important information.

Video Chat

Video chat was a tremendously underutilized technology tool until Covid. While adoption has skyrocketed, we are now starting to see more in-person events. When we have these in-person events, we need to make sure they are hybrid and include digital options. Having video chat available has helped to slash my gas budget as many more events can be done via Zoom. Mitigating a 150+ mile drive for a meeting is so helpful.

VBM (Vote-By-Mail)

Every campaign with large rural areas must prioritize a rigorous vote-by-mail program. The amount that mail ballots increase rural turnout is tremendous. VBM programs work incredibly well for those who favor higher voter turnout.

Direct Mail

Most of the time, especially in Nebraska, driving out to every farm is impossible. It's time-consuming and not at all efficient. A well-targeted direct mail program can help to get your message to these citizens. If you don't know how this is a good area, work with a consultant who understands rural communities. There is a wealth of information you can use to target individuals.

Phonebanks or Blitzes

Canvassing is by far the most effective way to gain votes in any community. However, in rural areas, this can be a logistical nightmare. One easy way to overcome this is to plan regular phone banks with your volunteers. It can also be helpful to blitz a town with a car full of canvassers who will knock out a small town in one trip.

Organizations

81

You don't have to start from scratch. In partisan work, consider your local Party Central Committee a vital resource. In nonpartisan work, consider plugging into other organizations. Great places to start are Farmers Unions, churches, Chambers of Commerce, or Rotary Clubs.

Show Up

The most important thing of all is to make sure you show up. Some months, my gas reimbursements have been larger than my paycheck. But when you show up, you prove that you are dedicated to that community. And then they will be dedicated to you.

Storytelling

"Storytelling reveals meaning without committing the error of defining it."

 --Hannah Arendt, political theorist, philosopher

Good storytelling captures the heart of complex issues in ways that can connect us all. When working in campaigns or advocacy, it's vital to capture a good story for talking to reporters, presenting at events, testifying at hearings, and advocating in your daily life.

First, you need to find your story. Here are some excellent questions to start discovering what that story is.

• What makes you passionate?

• Why are you here?

• What story best shows the problem?

• When have you felt frustrated?

Once you find that story, keep it simple, short, and focused. Then ask yourself: What is the key variable? If you had to take your story down to one page, what would it say?

Presentation

As you work to prepare your story, it's not just about what story you tell but how you tell it.

• Practice makes perfect

• Facial exercises

• Smile as big as you can for 30 seconds until it hurts. This exercise will help to warm up some of your facial muscles to help improve your sound. It will also help you to smile more as you talk.

When you smile as you talk, you will have a better sound, and people will find what you say more appealing.

• Open your eyes as wide as you can and raise your eyebrows, then close them as tight as you can. This facial stretch will help to ensure you look more alert and engaged as you talk.

• Open your mouth as wide as you can until it hurts and hold for 30 seconds. This practice will help to improve your ability to project. People always say that they are afraid they will overreact, but I've never seen anyone who does. You may feel you are too animated. But it will look normal for those at the back of a room or seeing you through a camera.

• Vocal Exercises

• Say the phrase, "Diction is done with the back of the teeth and the tip of the tongue." Start slow but then pick up your speed. This drill will help to increase your diction to the point that you can be more clearly understood.

• Singing is a powerful and fun tool to help you warm up. It doesn't matter if you are good or not; the singing will help warm up and flex your vocal cords. Stretch your voice by singing "ahhh" and work your way to as high of a tone as you can go. Do this three times. Then go as low as you can. This practice will help ensure you have flexibility in your voice and have a diverse range.

• Say your vowels in the most over pronounced way you can. "AEIOU" Repeat this 20 times. This exercise will increase your clarity

• Body Exercises

Your body will change based on how you prepare it to speak. It helps if you start by making sure it is ready to look ready to present to look comfortable, ready, and engaged. Warming your body up can also help to ensure that your sound is better. Good sound comes from throughout your entire body.

Touch your toes. This stretch will help ensure that you are ready to stand for a more extended period, prevent you from shuffling, and open up your body to produce a better sound.

The large majority of Americans have an issue with their posture. Roll your shoulders back 30 times, then forward 30 times. This exercise will help improve your posture to look more comfortable, engaged, and again you will sound better.

Dealing with Questions

Your story will not sit in a vacuum. People will ask questions, and frequently if they have something to lose from your story, they may push back.

• Trust Matters

• "I don't know but let me get back to you."

• Circle back to the point you want to make

• Reporters and legislators are looking for a line to quote, so always go back to what you want them to hear

• If you do feel uncomfortable, you can always refer them back to me

What to Avoid	What to Use
Impairment, Special Need, Deficit	Disability
Wheelchair-bound, Confined to a wheelchair Handicapped, Differently abled, Lame, Crip/Cripple/Gimp (when used by someone non-disabled), Spastic, Spaz, Physically challenged, Handicapable, Wheelz/Speed Racer/Speedy, Making speed limit/racer jokes	Wheelchair user, Disabled (preferred by most activists), People with Disabilities or PWDs, Cripple/Crip/Gimp (if someone self identifies this way), has (insert disability), Physically disabled
Retarded, Feeble-minded, Slow/Delayed, Developmental delay, Mentally deficient, Stupid, Dumb, Dimwitted, Idiot	Person with a Developmental Disability, Person with an Intellectual Disability, Person with Down Syndrome, Intellectually or Developmentally Disabled
Psychotic, Mad, Crazy, Demented, Mental, Loony, Nutjob, Nutso, Whacko, Psychopath, Crazed, Psycho, Deranged, Lunatic	Psychiatric disability/diagnosis, Mad* (reclaimed – there is a Mad pride movement), psychosocial disability, person with [specific diagnosis/disability]
Aspie (some do like this, but many abhor it), Person with autism	Autistic, Neurodivergent
Midget	Dwarf, little person

http://cdrnys.org/disability-writing-journalism-guidelines/

Communication Tools

Communication

One of the pillars of any campaign or cause-based organization is good communication. There are many tools to effectively take control of the messaging and have a powerful voice at the table.

Content Calendar

It's always helpful to start with an outline for a content calendar. This will help you to understand the broad themes and general direction you want to go. A Communications Plan with a solid Content Calendar needs to be at the heart of your efforts. A content calendar helps to ensure that we are not just reactive but proactive. We set an agenda of issues that we want to address and pre-develop content focused on it. This helps us to take control of the conversation and produce better content.

To do this, I use an Excel Document or a Google Sheet to get me started. Across the top, I will put the types of content I want. This could be a volunteer, a donation request, a policy statement, or shares from a related entity. Then I will have the first column be monthly themes. The second column is the date to post. The third column is the type of content. The fourth will be the content itself. This process helps you analyze content, stay focused, sort content, and keep to a schedule.

In the communications calendar, you want to ensure you plan several types of content. Types of content to include are: earned media opportunities, Letters to the Editor, Social Media Posts, Blog Posts, and Email Blasts.

Having a communications calendar can be helpful, especially with social media. With tools like Hootsuite (a social media software), you can write posts and determine when you want them to go up. Supplement these planned posts with reactive posts like photos of events. This pre-planned content allows board, interns, and volunteer participation in developing our message.

Email

Within the calendar, a significant focus should be email blasts. This will help keep members informed on a standard message and able to take quick action. The great thing about these messages is that if you have a quality CRM, it will be easier to track and respond.

Press Releases

Press releases are one of the most important tools in communicating with the press. A good press release can prompt a reporter to write a story on your issue. As our media system has changed, fewer reporters have to cover a wider array of stories. So reporters now have to look more towards the content you send them. Always getting them new content will increase your likelihood of getting stories published. This will also ensure that the story is looked at through the lens you want.

Text Blasts

One of the most significant new areas in outreach and community organizing is text tools. With response rates to phone calls falling you need to find new ways to connect with members. Texting allows for large-scale and personalized outreach. I've had many text blasts where someone thought it was only automated. When I followed up with a personalized message, they were shocked.

Integrated and Automated Follow-Ups

Large-scale reach and growth require automated follow-ups. Follow-ups tracked in your database can be even more powerful. If your current system does not automatically follow up with new sign-ups, this is an excellent tool to consider. If you don't follow up within the first 48 hours, you are more likely to lose volunteers.

Digital Application

Digital applications are the new space to innovate. They occupy a space that works well between in-person and digital. If you are looking to be on the next wave, then this hybrid space is one that you want to be in at the front edge of the curve.

Its clear digital applications will offer cost savings and increase efficiency. Features to consider are automatic follow-ups, a resource database, push alerts for direct action, and video access. While I'm still seeing where this tool will lead, I think this is a space to investigate and invest resources.

Direct Mail

Old-school direct mail is one of the most underestimated tools. I focus a lot on new techniques, but these old-school tools are pivotal. Direct mail has historically been an area that is held mainly for consultants. To democratize access to the process, we need more training on doing direct mail well.

Start by bringing in a talented graphic designer. The graphic designer will ensure that all your copy will shine, no

95

matter how crappy or great. Your piece will be a lot more effective if you get a design that looks good. While I'm always drawn in more by content, most people focus on how something looks more than what it says.

When writing copy, be clear, keep to core messaging, and avoid conflict. Then try to sketch out that content like you want it to look. Think about things like what size the piece will be, who will be looking at it, what it looks like on a kitchen table. Once you have your copy and a general idea, contact a graphic designer who knows what they are doing. While talented graphic designers are pricy they are a good investment.

Next, you need to find a good print shop to work with you. I mainly work with Unionist Printing because of their high-caliber service and flexibility. They have worked with me across numerous projects and have always been impressive. I've had several occasions where they even worked late into the night to help me get a piece out in time. Finding a shop that works well with you can be invaluable if you plan to do more of this type of work.

Another consideration is if you need a bulk mail permit. Although sometimes you can get another entity to use their bulk mail permit. Then think about the size of the piece you want and determine what that shipping cost will be.

Understanding the Business and Organizational

Structure of Change

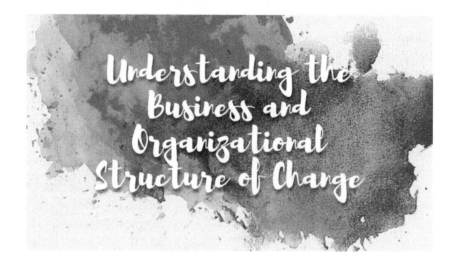

One of the least understood aspects of organizing is the business and organizational structures behind it. There are many types of structures that can be used for different parts of this work. That change doesn't just happen.

You want to start with a grassroots educational group building energy. But then you need good people elected to office, so you need PACs. Once those people are elected, they need knowledgeable staff to support them. When those government employees are spread too thin, they need help. So they need lobbyists who can provide expertise and guidance. So I want to talk a bit about some of these types of entities and a few highlights of what to be thinking about.

One of the entities I work with, GC Revolt, was created because we hit a wall. Helpful elected officials had started some great programs to grow renewable energy. However, even the best program doesn't mean anything if people don't use it. So we realized that we needed to help develop more projects. We were successful in developing more projects, but this led to new challenges. As we grew more, we began to hit caps that restricted more renewable energy development. So we had to go back to lobbying for changes to lift the caps.

To do this, we needed help from some good elected officials and their staff. But in their staff's extensive portfolio of issues, they needed extra expertise. That's where I would help to educate those policymakers and their staff members. I also help to keep the pieces moving on varying levels. Sometimes a change at a local utility means you are more likely to get a chance at a statewide level. As we've lifted these caps, we have seen the private market continue to boom. What this will look like for your work can vary.

Here are some of the types of entities you should have in mind:

(Disclaimer: I'm not an Attorney or a CPA, and you should not construe this as legal advice. Talk to a certified expert if you have questions. This is only for general information and their general role in organizing)

501 C3 Traditional Nonprofits

One of the largest benefits is that nonprofits have tax exemptions for contributions. This can be a tremendous benefit, especially for more significant donors. This is also beneficial because these benefits have few caps for donations. Nonprofits also have more access to foundations, government grants, and some corporate donations. The downside is public reporting, prohibitions on campaign activity, and limits around advocacy. While this is not a complete ban, you have to deal with limitations and the Significant Parts Test.

501(c)(4) Civic Groups and Social Welfare Organizations

101

This is the best type of entity for political action and lobbying. 501c4's are similar to 501c3's. The main difference is a broader ability for political and lobbying activities.

501(c)(6) Business Leagues and Chambers of Commerce

These usually are organizations that focus on industry-specific requirements. This could be lobbying for regulations to protect the industry from bad actors. Frequently, this will be to open more new business opportunities and sales. Sometimes this can also be to help get new government contracts. While they can do general educational activities like a 501c3, it will only be what is good for the industry.

Setup your Own Entity

As you think about the type of structure that you want to work with, there are many ways to structure your work. One of the most important, though, is to set up an entity for yourself. If

102

you have lots of contracts, significant liability, or are trying to maximize your resources, this can be helpful. This can be addressed with a simple Limited Liability Company (LLC). This creates important financial benefits like limited tax liability and better contract coordination. It can also help with limiting legal liability and improving your perceived legitimacy.

Building Powerful Digital Tools on a Budget

If you want to innovate in organizing, some of the best tools available are digital tools. The downside of this innovation is that you have to keep changing to keep up. But with some innovative techniques, you can do amazing things. We will discuss a few awesome digital tools/hacks that I've found helpful to reach a large audience.

Reaching a large audience is vital because the best program doesn't matter if no one knows about it. While the importance of reach is an issue for all causes, it is particularly prevalent in the disability community. Most disability professionals think the majority of people get services. But if you look at this graphic, you will see that it is far from the truth. Only 17% of people with IDD get the services they need 3% are on the Wait List, and 80% of people with IDD don't get anything. This means that we have a vast audience who doesn't know about the available services. So we need to be shouting that information from every rooftop we can find. We have the challenge to ensure we get out the information that we need to clearly and concisely.

But if you are only one person or a smaller team, it can be a challenge.

Despite this potential, senior staff continues to leave their digital tools to their newest staffer. This seems illogical in a world where tweets are quoted in news stories as much as press releases are. But still, we see senior staff who fail to evolve to leverage these powerful tools.

This failure to keep up with professional development around digital tools is troubling. If a doctor didn't keep up with the latest surgical practices, they would have difficulty keeping their job. Organizations that continue to ignore these latest practices will continue to fall behind. Yet, we fail to evaluate professionals who have roles in PR upon their digital knowledge.

Platforms

When talking about digital tools it's important to start with a quality platform. This needs to be a platform that fits your organizations needs. For instance, if you are fundraising and doing outreach consider a more integrated platform. Here are a few databases I tend to recommend.

Mailchimp

"MailChimp provides nonprofits with a 15% discount, as well as the option to get an additional 10% off if you authorize your account as a means of security. MailChimp boats robust marketing automation which makes sure your emails get to the right people at the right time. Some other features include being able to target your customers based on behavior, preferences, and more; automatically sending your emails at the same time in different time zones; triggering emails with a single API request; and accessing in-depth reporting insights. MailChimp also allows you to connect to your online store in order to create hundreds of e-commerce integrations as well as includes a drag-and-drop campaign builder. They even offer you the possibility to grow your audience with Facebook or Instagram ad campaigns. When

107

it comes to mobile options, MailChimp has got your covered. Check out more info about their suite of mobile apps."

Salesforce

"Salesforce.org Nonprofit Cloud is an integrated platform for nonprofits that allows you to manage your entire mission. Salesforce is the world's #1 CRM, and their community counts over 45,000 nonprofits. Nonprofit Cloud powers your mission by tracking and measuring impact in real-time, helping you raise more using insights from artificial intelligence on donors, and by taking every constituent on their own personal journey. Over 88% of Salesforce.org organizations have said that Salesforce helped them improve their ability to achieve their mission."

Salsa

"Over 10,000 nonprofits professionals work with Salsa. Salsa is a supporter engagement platform that encompasses nonprofit CRM, online fundraising, digital marketing and multichannel advocacy, including click to call, direct mail, and local/state/federal targeted messaging. Salsa is uniquely designed for nonprofits, and for those organizations already using a CRM such as Salesforce, Salsa offers an integration option, Salsa Engage.

By allowing organizations to combine all their offline and online supporter information in one place, Salsa enables you to easily segment, target, and report on your data visually. Salsa also automates regular tasks such as gift acknowledgments and targeted list building, includes a library of emails and forms for jumpstarting campaigns, and offers multiple channels for training and support."

EveryAction

EveryAction is a unified nonprofit CRM that powers both online and offline fundraising, as well as advocacy efforts, volunteer programs, and grants management. Its unique features include one-click contributions via email and a network of millions of saved donor profiles to help nonprofits raise more money. It is used by over 5,000 organizations.

Nationbuilder

NationBuilder is a cloud-based website, database and fundraising solution designed for nonprofits to connect with their communities and scale their organizations. It includes features to identify key supporters, turn them into donors, accept and process online donations and enable peer-to-peer outreach. Dynamic user profiles are updated with every interaction and automatically sync with public social media information. The solution can be used globally by nonprofits, advocacy groups, membership and alumni organizations, and associations of all sizes.

Asset Mapping Process with Form

We used Google Forms and Sheets to create this in a short period. This helps you easily update your information.

110

This process is also helpful to see the geographic layout, especially in rural areas. You need to understand your spread of resources. It doesn't matter for someone in Scottsbluff if you have ten staff in Lincoln. It will be hard to get them to travel hundreds of miles unless it's absolutely necessary. This means they have a resource they can use and understand what is near them for families.

Steps

Set up a Google Form with the survey questions you want. Questions like what is your Agency Name, Address, Phone, Email, and Services Provided. Then export these answers to a spreadsheet in Google Sheets. Next, click on get Add On's in the menu. Next, you will need to select Map my Sheet. This will walk you through creating an interactive Google Map.

This will give you a better idea of your spread of resources. It may take some formatting work but is worthwhile. The end result should be easy to share and easy to update by using the Google Form.

How to Schedule 100 One-on-One Meetings in 1 Hour of Work

The heart of all fundraising and organizing work is about developing deep relationships. There is no more extraordinary tool to develop relationships than the One-on-One Meeting. Any community-centered work should have these types of interactions as a key focus. However, the issue with these meetings is they take a lot of time. So how transform this vital old-school technique to use in the modern world?

In his book Believer, David Axelrod, Obama's Campaign Manager, says there are two types of operatives. Old School Operatives use their gut feeling and personal knowledge. In comparison, New School Operatives use Data and Technology. I'm a firm believer that the most significant potential is in the synergy between the two.

You can evolve this old-school technique with personalization and lightening fast reach by using your database. Some programs overuse this. But the occasional carefully crafted use can be powerful. I've used this powerful hack to set up over 100 One-On-One Meetings in an hour.

I used a short, personalized email script saying," (your name) let's get coffee to talk about the future of The Arc." I would connect this to a link to Calendly, a tool that schedules meetings in your Google Calendar with no work. The brevity in these emails is vital because it makes it feel as if it is personal and not another bulk email. I have been surprised by the positive reactions to this. I found lifelong members who had never talked to a staffer.

A strength of this technique is that it cut down on the back-and-forth emails.

Me "When are you free?"

Donor "Those times don't work for me."

Me "How about Tuesday?"

Donor "What is this about again?"

Instead, prospects pick a time from your Google Calendar openings. This also allows you to restrict times for other projects easily. The first time I did this, I didn't use Calendly and drowned in back-and-forth emails. Without Calendly, I was overloaded with scheduling emails. This meant missed opportunities and connections. With Calendly, they clicked, and it was on my calendar.

In these one-on-one meetings, I would share my story and ask for theirs.

Then I would ask, "What do you think the future of (the organization) should be?" You then figure out where that fits in your strategic plan. With this values alignment, you can transition into a natural fundraising ask.

If you need help to find your story. Here are some excellent questions to start discovering what that story is.

• What makes you passionate?

• Why are you here?

• What story best shows the problem?

• When have you felt frustrated?

Petitions

Many of the platforms we discussed earlier have petition capabilities. Digital Petitions are great ways to get a lot of people to take a quick little action. Set up a Google Form with your petition language if you don't have a platform with these capabilities.

But it doesn't end with that action. You need to keep educating your contacts by emailing them more info as you go. Once you get the digital petition, push it to your email list and bulk share on social media wherever you can

Social Media Bulk Sharing

Social Media is a powerful tool, but it can be hard to spread things around limiting algorithms. An easy action is to join and/or create Facebook Groups around your topic. You can then share your posts from your main page to those groups. Don't be afraid to overshare. There is no such thing.

Hashtags

Finding the right hashtag is part science and part art. You can look at popular hashtags to help boost your reach. You can also start your own unique hashtag. Whatever hashtag you choose, use it consistently. If you have the same hashtags across platforms, it will help to track similar posts.

Bulk Following

Followers are key to expanding reach for Twitter, Instagram, and Tik Tok. The easiest way to increase your followers is to start following others. From a general follow, you can expect approximately 10% of accounts will follow you back. As always, start with your personal contacts. Then look at who has used certain hashtags or follows similar organizations. You can use these as prospect lists to begin following and hope they follow back.

Surveys with Google Form

The danger of large groups is that it can be harder to hear everyone. Many times there are a few "loud" voices who may dominate conversations. To mitigate this, you want to look at tools that ensure everyone has a chance to express their opinions. A great way to do this is with surveys. This will help you to understand your organization and update or grow your contact list.

Questions to ask:

Name, Age, Address, Email, Phone, Member?

Employer

What is your role in the organization?

What is our mission?

What's the best way to contact you?

Are you regularly updated on our work?

Do you feel your contribution is important?

Are there ample pieces of training available?

Is it clear how funds are used?

Are we geographically inclusive?

What is the biggest thing we could improve?

Anything else you need to understand about your members

List Buying

List buying is a great way to increase reach quickly. Although you may have a high flake rate, this is a great tool to get to many people rapidly. As you reach out, then you can follow up to create an ongoing dialogue.

Paid Adds

Paid digital ads are another way to target an area quickly. While there is a cost, you get a significant return on your investment. If you direct them to a signup form, you can continue to contact them without continuing to pay for more ads.

$100 Budget for Best Reach

All of these tools sound great, but you may wonder about budget or staff time. So here are two barebones sample budgets to use these tools. The first one is a $100 Budget and 1 hour of staff time per week with Significant Reach.

Service	Month	Annual
Mailchimp	$ 0.00	$ 0.00
Google Tools Free	$ 0.00	$ 0.00
Calendly	$ 6.00	$ 72.00
Grammarly Free	$ 0.00	$ 0.00
Ripl free create graphics	$ 0.00	$ 0.00
Paid social media	$ .00	$ .00

Here is a $1000 a Year Budget

Service	Month	Annual
Nationbuilder Starter	$ 29.00	$ 348.00
Google Tools Business	$ 12.00	$ 144.00
Calendly	$ 6.00	$ 72.00
Grammarly Pro	$ 12.00	$ 144.00
Ripl create graphics	$ 9.99	$ 118.98
Paid social media	$ 14.00	$ 168.00
Total		$ 995.98

Vote By Mail

Campaigns are constantly becoming more data-centered in a race to mobilize voters. This leads to highly partisan messages that influence who we elect. Which makes us question who our elected officials are serving. But with this in mind, we have to take a new perspective on how we campaign. No longer is it as much about changing the minds of people in the middle but turning out your supporters. To do that, some of the most valuable tools are direct voter contact and vote by mail (VBM). In my college senior seminar, I took a deep look at how effective these tools were. If you want to read more look here

https://www.linkedin.com/pulse/effectiveness-direct-contact-vote-mail-efforts-nebraska-edison/

But I wanted to chat about some highlights here. I wanted to research the effects of direct voter contact on Nebraska Elections. Green and Gerber (2000) laid down the basis for understanding these effects I wish to expand upon. They approach it through a nonpartisan lens. I wanted to continue this research only with a partisan focus. How does VBM help your candidate or cause and not just raise voting generally (which you could argue supports all democracy)? While others had explored VBM before, I found previous studies too narrowly focused. Nebraska was a great place to look since at the time, we had only seen significant expenditures on VBM on one side of the aisle. This has since changed but gave me a great area to look at for the time.

The question I was trying to answer was "What, is the effect of direct voter contact on Nebraska Vote by Mail turnout, particularly in rural areas?"

It is hard to eliminate variables to understand this issue clearly. But I was able to find some clear conclusions. I thought that I would find that "Voters contacted directly more likely to VBM in the next election than those not contacted." And that

"The increased likelihood of Vote By Mail will not be as high in more rural areas.

I picked several test counties to understand main divisions. I picked test counties to account for size, location, and voting history. I divided small rural (Blaine and Cherry), mid-size rural (Adams and Buffalo), and metropolitan counties (Lancaster and Omaha).

The total VBM registration is flat in these areas, both in the test counties and across the state. This is important to ensure increased voter registration doesn't affect the results, which calls into question the efficiency of voter registration efforts in electoral politics.

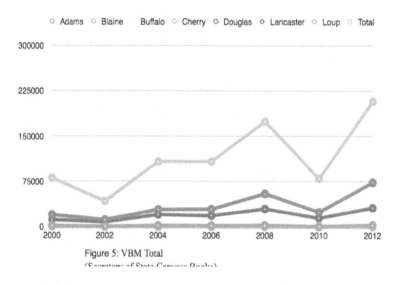

Figure 5: VBM Total
(Secretary of State Canvass Books)

As you can see in the chart, this research was very helpful in supporting part of my hypothesis. Direct contact efforts focused on VBM are highly effective. Especially effective are direct contacts are in rural communities. Rural communities staying potential outpaces semi-rural communities. Both rural and semi-rural community efforts are more effective than urban areas. While it didn't fully support my hypothesis, it warrants more investigation into the effect on rural communities.

Some other notable findings in this study include:

124

- [ ] When you have good large coordinated efforts, you get more bang for your buck.

- [ ] Nebraska's Secretary of State had a difficult to access public data at the time, but they've gotten a lot better.

- [ ] That different types of contact have different effects. I'll talk about more about the Ladder of Engagement. But I have to note that much of the research on types of contact comes from Green, Gerber, and Parry's research.

- [ ] Lastly, that there is a spending cap where this direct contact stops being as effective. I'm hopeful because this means that money influences but isn't the only factor in races.

Turnout Tools Study

From a young age, I have been interested in Membership Organizations. Collaborating is key to creating civic and community change. Yet typically, I have been an outlier amongst my generation. Frequently, I have heard the question posed, "How do we get the young people?" In a tone-deaf attempt to listen.

Organizations like these have been on the decline for quite a long time now. "In the past two decades, Rotary down 20%, Jaycees down 64%, Masons down 76%. Recalling de Tocqueville's observation about our clubs' role in civil society, this decline represents a tangible loss to the community. The question remains, 'Where do we go from here?" According to http://michaelbrand.org/why-our-service-clubs-are-dying/

My answer has been focused on how to leverage various community organizing tools. Nonprofit outreach is turning increasingly to new tools in the modern day.

I am the Executive Director for The Arc of Nebraska. The Arc of Nebraska aims for a more inclusive world for people with intellectual and developmental disabilities. Like many other organizations over the last 60 years, we have had a decrease in engagement. But with some of the tools, we will discuss, we have turned that membership trend around.

I was brought in to modernize our organization and help adapt for new generations.

What follows are some case studies of the organizing tools we have attempted and the results. The dinner is our largest annual event. Last year, with email and online signup, we were able to add approximately 100 seats to 273 seats. This year we had 296 seats ordered.

Email

Emails 2,116

27.04% opened

3.61% clicked

2,116 Emails

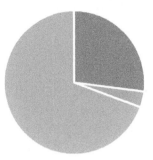

- Opened Emails
- Clicked Emails
- Sent Emails

An email is a quick tool that has significantly increased our communication efficiency. Over the last year, this has become a key base of ours. While we had previously had small email blasts with lists of a few dozen people bounced around, we did not have nearly so powerful a list. The customization has also been a significant addition to events, actions, and advocacy.

Texts

Initial Messages 559

Initial Responses 76

Yes 37 7%

No 42 7%

Texting is a new tool for us. Having just begun this year, we are working to understand the effects and implications. The engagement levels have been significantly higher, although our reach is not quite as broad yet. The personal interactions that we have had off this have been fantastic in engaging new members who have not previously participated via email.

Social Media

47 Going

132 Interested

5,500 Reached

73 Ticket Clicks

We have had an active Facebook page for a while but have been working to increase the quality of the content. At the same time, we are balancing the concern that we may excessively increase the quantity of content.

130

We have increased the reach significantly and engagement, particularly by targeting Facebook Live. However, as Facebook becomes more inundated with content, we are still adapting to the constantly evolving methods.

Direct Mail 6,888

While undoubtedly one of our most expensive methods, it is still one of the highest response items. The overlap with our other tools in this category is significant. While digital tools offer substantial benefits, the vital nature of direct mail is still painfully clear.

Calls 284

It seems we had some increase related to the event calls. However, we did not see a significant boost with the overlap from other methods for the work level. Clearer A/B testing is necessary to determine the actual effect of this. I would like to dig more into the relationship between email and text response.

Lastly, we have a chart of our social media reach to give you a general idea of the basic demographics of our audience.

We have a powerful lean towards women as mothers are our main drivers. The age trends from this event are significantly down from our general membership, which lies more in the 40+ range.

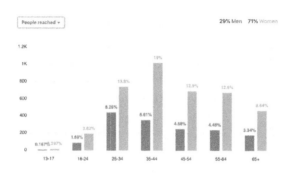

A more recent campaign has been our #EndtheList Campaign. Nebraska has 2300 families waiting on services which have been waiting on this list on average for 6-8 years. While we commonly like to believe that our government takes care of people with disabilities. But the truth is we don't, and we haven't for a long time. The Waiting List has been an issue that The Arc of Nebraska has been building momentum around and educating people about for decades. However, it's frequently been hamstrung by over-complication, failures to engage the community, and failure to properly educate stakeholders. Throughout this campaign, we used various tools to help overcome many of these issues with minimal resources.

• Automated follow up

• Funnel

• Education

First of all, this issue is frequently used to divide our community by splitting families of those who get services and making them fearful of those who don't have services.

They like to pit people with autism versus those with Down syndrome—younger people with disabilities versus older people with disabilities. So, we decided that we would take a broader look. We could broaden and strengthen our coalition by bringing together different parts of the disability community and finding innovative solutions to critical problems that helped raise all tides.

Levels of Engagement

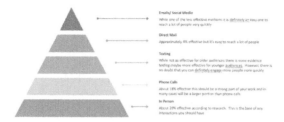

Petition Drive

With our petition drive, we gathered over 1600 petition signatures. These signers were at the core of this effort. This was an essential engagement tool, created pressure, and captured press attention. The National Press Coverage amped up the pressure on the administration. Most importantly, this was just Step One. This funneled to massively increased engagement, membership sign-ups, and donors.

Waiver Study

When diving into our values, we saw that we needed to have multiple levels of the conversation. Most people can only remember a sentence. Some can hear a presentation. Some will have personal conversations with their Senators. This helped to serve as a base document to center the movement and set a more specific direction. This helped to capture the stories and show how policy relates to stories.

Community Presentations

We did a series of presentations across the state to educate and arm our members. Most people don't understand the issues involved because they are intentionally complicated. We need to do a better job ensuring overwhelmed parents can, in a limited time, really comprehend and quickly act.

These in-person conversations also allow for dialogue and community forming. Another helpful tool we have been using more frequently is Facebook Live. The benefits Live offers are families who are busy during a presentation can watch it later. They also can be easily shared.

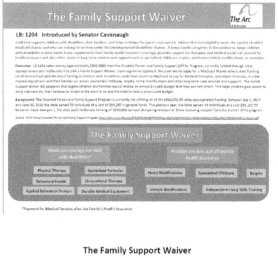

Legislative Hearings

When you have direct action to tie to your calls, it increases drive. For this campaign, we tied the policy proposals from our study into everything. This started with educational presentations, hearings and lead to legislation. We also connected the stories straight into these hearings.

The intersection of Old and New

One of my favorite minds in this space to look at is the work of David Axelrod, who was Obama's Campaign Manager. In Axelrod's book Believer, discusses two types of staffers. Old school staff goes off of gut feeling, and the new school focus on data. Neither produces the optimal results without the other. You may also want to consider using separate tools with separate audiences. For instance, direct mail may be more effective with older audiences. Or to find ways to combine them more powerfully than either of them individually.

Cause as a Driver

Pew Research tells us that nowadays, people want to be spiritual but not "religious." This means that they want to be values-centered but not necessarily institution-centered. Like they want to be close to God, but they don't see that path through the church. This Values-driven mentality is more important than ever.

This means small actions, fundraisers, new nonprofits, and personalized actions are more important. These actions also need to be Digital and Timely with stories that connect deeply. I find that if you can understand this deep connection, you can get younger volunteers. These volunteers will likely not just take a task but a whole project. This leads to far better engagement and returns that will open up new doors.

Free Content as Driver

I have found that it can be invaluable to show expertise or value that offers substance. This leads to deeper connections move people beyond individual actions.

This type of material can help you grow an audience and a true fan base with deep dedication. This quality content will also open

138

doors by being more likely shareable. Deep pieces or unique perspectives can sometimes take off. Most recently, a thoughtful post led to the interest and support of a minor celebrity.

I'm also a fan of this type of free content because it allows you to help master the messaging on an issue. It's tough to convince reporters to write exactly what you want. But with free content like a blog or resource guide, you can set things up exactly how you want. This means that you can do a deep dive into complex issues. It can also be helpful if you want to change the conversation. For instance, I was working on a bill about the liability of teachers who use improper restraint. The teachers union had a good grassroots outreach campaign to convince people it was an issue of teacher safety.

But they were missing our side of the conversation. They failed to acknowledge restraint is mostly used on students with disabilities and students of color. So we produced several materials and videos to help educate citizens and legislators. This was significant in changing the conversation and getting our members' voices heard.

These articles can also benefit your web presence. In particular if you leverage your Search Engine Optimization (SEO). Otherwise you may miss a connection from Google Searches on an issue. We've found this very true on the issue of restraint. If you make this a practice for your key issues you will connect with more individuals on a variety of issues.

Specialty

Areas

Organizing is ultimately always dependent upon the community. The most common way for organizers to fail is by applying an unmodified model to a community. Instead, you need to think through and adapt your tools to fit your community authentically.

No matter how many years of experience you have, you must always start by listening. Once you have listened and understood your community, you can begin to organize. This is key before you begin to customize your methodology to fit your community. If you don't follow through on this initial step, then you have missed the point. It should not be your goal to empower yourself but to empower those you are working to organize.

Therefore, I want to take the time to talk about some specific types of communities. I've chosen communities I have expertise in, and organizers frequently find challenging. While these won't apply across every community, they have themes that you can use to think through.

"What makes community organizing especially attractive is the faith it places in the ability of the poor to make decisions for themselves."

Paul Wellstone

Rural Communities

In Nebraska, we have a strong history of grassroots movements. These movements surprise many in their ability to topple traditional power structures. While some may find this surprising, if you know Nebraska's history, it should be expected. We have a Non-Partisan Unicameral, Publicly Owned Power and history of diverse leadership. Nebraska is a divided state – politically, geographically, and culturally. Maybe the only thing we can all rally behind is our football team (Go Big Red!).

To overcome these divides, we must invest in organizing and developing new communities. I've spent years organizing rural Nebraska. During this time, I've picked up some useful tools and knowledge. Here are some lesson's I've learned working in rural communities:

The values in a community are vital to understanding folks' perspectives and what they hold dear. The best way to inspire true passion for change in a community is to capture these ideas. Tradition, faith background, town pride, school pride, or a hope for a brighter tomorrow may be part of these values. Your understanding and respect of residents' values determine how effective you will be.

I saw this gathering petition signatures for Medicaid Expansion in a small town. When I say small, they had a gas station and a bar, and that was about it. So, after a few hours of standing at the gas station and knocking on doors with little luck, I decided to go into the bar. I walked in and found a few tables of guys. So, I started chatting with one about the town and the game playing. This, of course, led to talking about the Huskers. I'm always surprised how that Husker pride can develop new friends across Nebraska.

This created a bond, and other people from other tables started to hop in. Needless to say, I walked out of there with more signatures than I had gotten in hours out in the hot sun.

146

"Every moment is an organizing opportunity, every person a potential activist, every minute a chance to change the world."
Dolores Huerta

Rural communities frequently have organizations for change built into their core. With few people in your community, it increases the importance of working together. Church Bake Sales and PTA Meetings have already built this mentality into their DNA.

The structure to create change already exists, so all you have to do is tap into it.

I saw this in a small county central committee started by one passionate church choir member. She knew who to call and what to ask them. She made short work of getting everyone into their positions. A guy with a truck wasn't big on talking to people who were excellent at getting out yard signs. An older lady couldn't walk, but she had lots of time and was happy to make phone calls. She was plugged in and had been part of all of these

147

events and organizations for years. This can be an easy and natural organizing experience if you can just tap into that type of network.

Most organizations are used to having key members in larger communities. But in smaller communities, a key community member can have a huge voice. They bring the authority that you need to establish credibility and interest. If you can find even one of these key community members, you may see some organizational momentum.

In a rural race, I consulted on the name of a few key endorsers who worked absolute magic. When we had them do radio ads, we saw quick connections built throughout the county.

Key institutions can play just as vital of a role as key community members. These institutions need not be official in nature. They could be the Saturday morning coffee crew, a legion group, the local Rotary, or a book club. This change requires a local group of dedicated people. These people can

148

become a small group of thoughtful, committed citizens who can change the world.

There have been several early morning coffee groups that have invited me to speak. These groups can help you to find some excellent volunteers. While distributing information, they can also help spread it through their powerful networks, whether that information is who is looking to sell some land or talking about a great new candidate or cause.

Folks always care about the local economic drivers that power their community. Economic drivers include groups like farmers, local factories, and business organizations. Make sure to research the local area and prioritize a focus on those groups. In most towns in Nebraska, I find it super helpful to be able to talk about corn and soybeans. If you know the basics and can keep track of the latest prices, you have a great piece to dive into the conversation.

In many rural areas, a small number of families can control a significant amount of the land and property. Tapping into these families can often ensure a large amount of local support.

Many organizers seem not to understand that one of the best places for change is a church. If you look through history, many movements were powered by churches. For instance, the civil rights movement was organized in lots of church basements. Until organizers understand this, the urban-rural divide will continue to grow.

For many towns, Sunday church is one of the universal activities they have. This shared experience can be helpful to gain broader community support, especially if you have a key church leader who can help to champion your issue.

When identifying churches, look towards mainline denominations' national statements. Many of these churches will have helpful key statements of belief or doctrine you can use. I find this can be a good pathway to start a discussion on your issue.

I grew up talking with people in my church and they would ask me about my life and my interests. Inevitably that would lead towards discussions around my interest in political issues. I would be shocked to find out how many of them were on the other side of the political aisle from me. I struggled with this for quite some time. But then I realized the world isn't black and white. From the common base of our faith I found far more that bound us together than separated us. This mentality has been core in my work as I find new ways to bring people together and expand my insights.

Although my experience comes significantly from regions where farmers are key economic drivers. There are many rural communities where farmers aren't the main economic drivers. But even in those situations farmers are still significant assets. For instance you may want to use their land for an event or barn signs. Many times, farmers have several tracts of land. This can be helpful to garner spaces for signs on multiple key roads.

Many people from non-rural areas characterize rural areas using broad strokes. You can't just use a one-size-fits-all strategy. Remember each small community has its own identity. So always remember to make your model work for the community instead of forcing the community into a model. Which is why, I remind you, this is not a comprehensive list but a good beginning framework.

By nature, people fear the "other." If you aren't a member of the community, you risk becoming construed as the other. The best way to avoid this issue is to be ready to hop into your car and get out into these communities as much as you can. This time will familiarize you with their values and interests. But it will also help community members to know and trust you.

Without listening and building trust you will be facing an uphill challenge. I've seen many well-intentioned organizers who try to direct instead of empower. If you are directing you likely aren't focusing on the communities voice. Instead you are at risk of having your voice really taint that community interest.

Instead, you need to start by listening and understanding. Only then can you find a shared path forward.

These key features can help you identify how to change a rural community. The potential for change in these communities is huge if you can identify these key aspects.

Faith Organizing

Within community organizing, a faith organizing is frequently ignored. Being a Christian (Presbyterian), a former Youth Group Director, a former church elder, having worked for the National Presbyterian Church, graduate with Political Science and Religion degrees, a faith organizer, a political staffer, a community organizer, and broadly involved community member this status quo concerns me. These communities can be vital to creating large scale community change.

(I wanted to note I will tend to focus on Christian Faiths as that is a strong majority in many of the areas that I've worked in. I will speak broadly of general traditions that may need more nuance.)

We forget that Jesus was, at the base, a community organizer. He advocated for the poor, the sick, children, and the oppressed. He fought the rich, flipped tables of injustice, and started a revolution. Christians are reformers centered on justice. So we will discuss tools to start organize in faith communities near you.

Tools for Addressing Pastors

When addressing pastors, keep in mind their backgrounds. Typically, pastors are highly educated with advanced degrees. When addressing them, references to theologians, scholarly work, and well-backed research is vital. Logical and well-researched discussion helps to inform their decisions and actions. If you can provide these resources, it is far more likely they will be willing to help you.

They are normally holding a diverse community together. This makes it difficult to speak on controversial issues. They are afraid this will mean that they may alienate members. That fear is both for their members spiritual well being and the health of their church. They want to keep their members together instead of heading for the church down the street.

So, help to offer them cover. Examples include:

Citing support from a national entity.

Bringing more people to their Church.

Helping to publish a positive news story about them.

Bringing other pastors in the community to the table.

Sermon Pitching

There is lots of training in pitching stories to reporters. But this skill is easily translated to reach another audience. Much like reporters pastors have to come up with a lot of content. Sermon Pitching allows you to help feed them good new content. Just like with pitching reporters you need to make their job easier. If you give pastors quality academic, biblical, and societal resources they will likely preach on it.

Connect the Story

A good story can connect your cause in a powerful way. The Bible does this frequently by using parables to illustrate concepts. We need to do the same thing and remind people what that story looks like today. Remind people what Christ-like actions mean now. We need to join those trying to feed the

157

hungry, heal the sick, and care for the children. These types of stories will mobilize a church to action.

Tangibles

Faith communities prioritize different benefits than many organizations. But churches still need members, money, and community support. These things help them to carry out their mission on a larger level. So when you can help them with these goals it makes a difference. In particular if you can find that way to help them amplify their message to connect with more people.

For instance, I talk to a lot of church leaders about creation care (environmental issues). While most pastors see this as part of their calling, they see it financially prohibitive. So, I talk about how living their mission can help their bottom line also. If they insulate their windows or have a heated sanctuary floor their can be huge financial savings. Or for a church that invests in solar with the right financing they can save money in

158

the short and long term. When they see the impact of these changes in their budgets it can change minds quickly. This will help as members see these benefits and begin to consider similar things in their own homes.

Biblical References

Biblical stories and quotes are essential. We have to tie our message to a Biblical base text. That said, it is important to look at these in context through a historical-critical lens. Which means remembering that humans wrote the Bible with a variety of goals in mind. Then what was written has been translated several times. Each translation you have people with different purposes and qualities of interpretation. It's like a game of Telephone. The childhood game where you have people line up and whisper a phrase down the line. The longer the line the more your phrase will change. So try to use translations that keep this in mind like the New Revised Standard Version. The largest of these was the compilation of what we now know as the

Bible happened at The Council of Nicaea. It was basically a convention where leaders decided what books would become part of canon and which would be rejected.

So with creation care issues, I start with Genesis 1. "In the beginning God created..." It reminds us of all the things God created and that we were put here to be caretakers of that creation. I also like to use the story of Noah and the flood like victims of climate change. Since many churches do disaster relief work this can be a great connection.

Theological References

There are many good theologians to read. These thinkers help to frame much of the dialogue in a faith community. A few good theologians to start with: Merton, Augustine, Aquinas, Calvin, Luther, Knox, Bonhoeffer, Barth, Moltmann, Cox, McFague. It's always helpful to have a quote from one of these folks up your sleeve to start a dialogue.

These theologians will provide you more insight into their thoughts and maybe even your thoughts. For instance, I'm a Presbyterian who looks significantly to Calvin. But I also identify a lot with the writings of John Wesley, who is a key Methodist theologian.

Disability Community Organizing

I have also had a significant background working in the disability community. This is an interesting community that has some surprising things that can split or bind them together. I've been privileged to serve as the Executive Director for The Arc of Nebraska. The Arc of Nebraska promotes and protects the human rights of people with intellectual and developmental disabilities and actively supports their full inclusion and participation in the community throughout their lifetimes.. We've played a significant role on disability issues across Nebraska and the world. This has been due to several key factors:

This strength has come from a strong base of local parents, self-advocates, professionals. In the 1950's these partnerships were established as part of the deinstitutionalization movement. They created a strong federation of local chapters to establish the state organization. With local, state, and national entities they have created tremendous change.

163

Relationships built over 60 years ago have created a rich history of changemakers. For instance, I'm in a coffee group started 60 years ago with people in our roles. Some things have changed. It started off with all night debates over a bottle of bourbon. Now it's a 7 am Monday morning coffee. But some things haven't changed. The close collaboration and discussion keeps many things moving.

Historic leaders like Wolf Wolfensberger (Internationally renowned academic in the disability world) partnered with Bill Wills (Community Organizer Executive Director of The Arc of Nebraska) and Dr. Frank Menolascinoa (Mover and Shaker) to create this powerful partnership that shows how change can happen if you partner academics with community organizers. While I never would want to be an academic, I deeply value the information that they provide.

There are a few key academics who I still look to. They provide me with the latest research, and ideas well grounded in

164

research. This helps me as I look towards what we should be working on. Their thoughts help to inspire how things should work. Then I work to mobilize the people and convince those in power to make it happen.

This coalition was and still is very broad. We have members with a wide set of values, ideas, and perspective. But they have something stronger that binds them together. In the chart below you can see the framing that they used to hold this coalition together.

(Out of the Darkness and Into the Light, Robert Schalock)

TABLE 2.1
Major Sociocultural Values in Nebraska and Their Positive Action Implications

Prominent Values	Positive Action Implications
1. Law and order; constitutionalism	Service as a right Retarded as "citizens"
2. Middle-church Protestantism (service orientation; guilt motivation)	Confrontation with dehumanization Normalization
3. Protestant ethic	Schooling, training, work
4. Fiscal conservatism; nonduplication of services	Cost-benefit rationale Generic agency integration
5. Rugged individualism: mutual assistance	Citizen advocacy Consumer-professional partnership
6. Private enterprise	Competitive institution standards Consumer-professional partnership
7. Frontier pragmatism	Realistic limits to demands
8. Local initiative and control	Dispersal of services Funding partnerships Consumer-professional partnership

much of our devaluing language in the past, had a tremendous impact.

Citizen! The word evokes mental images of the star-spangled banner waving, of "bombs bursting in air," cymbals clashing, the Fourth of July, and the armed forces parading by in their glory. Fine! As human affairs go, these images have some endurance, and one can build a program on them.

With the word *citizen*, one immediately associates civic rights such as those to free movement, to free communication, and to services. We could readily demonstrate that these rights had been persistently, and largely unnecessarily, denied to the residents of our institutions. The constitution of every state in the Union mi

I've been working on this book on and off for around seven years. But I wouldn't be doing this work justice if I did not include a bit about the radical shifts we have seen since Covid. Community organizing has become radically different nearly overnight. We went from in-person, to entirely virtual, to now some sort of new hybrid. Every day it seems things are still changing depending on the latest stage of the Covid Pandemic. While there are still many things that work the same, many things have radically changed. I wanted to offer a few lessons I have learned working through these changes.

Embrace the Change

You are converting an airplane as you are flying it. You have also been doing so for a long time at this point. The things that have worked in the past may work, or they may not. Don't be afraid to try something and fail (even things that have failed in the past may work now). There is no one with more pandemic organizing than anyone else.

Brevity to Beat Zoom Fatigue

Zoom was a fantastic tool that went from a technology some were adopting to a universal standard overnight. Now we have all logged hundreds or thousands of hours in Zooms and are tired of it. In the face of this, the best thing a lot of times is to cut a meeting short when it doesn't need to go on. Or even considering canceling if there isn't much content.

Leverage Trusted Sources and Influencers

We have always had key community members who establish legitimacy and trust. They can spread information through extensive networks quickly. However, now these key community members frequently look a bit different. We have seen grassroots leaders who started social media resource pages become trusted messengers. These folks can be some of the most effective tools in your arsenal. Sit down (physically or virtually) with these key players early on, recruit them to your side, and talk to them regularly.

Email and CRM

It is no longer optional to have a top-of-the-line email program. Any organization without a quality integrated CRM is flopping on an important front. They need to evolve from Excel to a quality database tool as soon as possible. Becasue a well-developed email list can enable you to connect quickly with volunteers and your larger audience. That said, with almost everyone doing email in some way now, you need to find your unique voice.

Authenticity

In so many ways, Covid has been a catalyst for change that was coming anyway. One of these major shifts is that authenticity is more important to cut through the noise. People have so much information coming at them they can't keep up. They want information to feel authentic and genuine. Content that feels scripted and pre-planned gets lost. So, keep it unique and let your voice really shine through. Also don't be afraid to be a bit silly or raw.

170

Phone Calls

While phones are a staple of community organizing, they are now more critical than ever. People want a more direct connection. Phone calls are often more welcome now then pre pandemic. If you are willing to just chat people can be excited to connect with someone new.

Texts

I was skeptical of the role of texting in community organizing for a long time. But with better tools developed for large scale texting it's become invaluable. With the super high read and response rates, it's a great way to have some sort of actual interaction with a person. You can also actually interact with so many people. This is great, especially for senior leaders or candidates, as people will be surprised when you respond that it is actually you.

Facebook Live

This is another piece that was heading this way pre-pandemic. The importance of video content is now so undeniable. There are several things I like about Facebook Live you don't see in other platforms. There is an extra bump in natural reach, it's easier to interact with people, you can connect to events as reminders, and it's automatically recorded in a fashion that is easy to share for viewing live or later.

Social Media Infographics

People are overwhelmed and exhausted. They have so much information at their fingertips they can't handle it. It's important to get a good shareable graphic to get a manageable bit to people quickly and clearly.

Keep At It. I don't care who you are. This is hard. You will struggle at points, but persistence is so crucial.

Stories

I wanted to talk about a few stories because stories ground us in the face of adversity. Since you will face challenges you need to find your compass to keep you ethically on track. So here are some of the stories that keep me grounded.

Sometimes I get cocky. I like to think that I am an activist, a mover, a shaker that has come to be as such on his own. I want to think, as many do you, that I have pulled myself up by my bootstraps. But as you can see in most stories, that is far from the truth. We all owe an outstanding debt of gratitude to many people who have helped get us where we are. Not only with those we have interacted with but upon the generations of leaders that have come before. These stories inspire and drive me to create change.

The true stories of bravery are not those of men in power but those who stand up in the face of overwhelming odds for what is right. They stand for justice and righteousness regardless of repercussions.

175

I remember reading [Studs Terkel's] "Working" when it first came out and just finding that very powerful. I was going into community organizing. What stuck was to reveal the sacredness of ordinary people's lives. That everybody has a story. And I think Studs is terrific at drawing out that shimmering quality of people's everyday struggles.

Barack Obama

I share these stories because, ultimately, there is something that no training can truly teach you in the previous sections. Ethics, character, friendship, dedication, passion, and a sense of divine guidance is necessary for the difficult work that lay ahead of you. I could not write a real guide to organizing without including stories like these.

Tick Tock

One of the best stories I know of comes from my family. As I've spent more time looking at these stories of bravery, I've realized rarely do they happen in a vacuum. Servant leaders build and grow over generations. They have been raised with stories of their parent's and grandparents actions. Understanding these trends helps you to see the whole picture of who that person is and what that change really means.

Families teach values that last far longer than we might ever know. Whether it is nature or nurture, there is a trend of families who care more about others than about themselves.

I begin with the story of the Tic Tock, a restaurant near the Southside of Chicago in the early 1900s. I don't have a tremendous amount of reference for much of the story other than what has been handed down and boxes of receipts and paperwork. The kind that you put away in case an audit was to come along, and the taxman were to say I have a question. Or perhaps you keep them just in case you don't know why, but my grandparents and uncle kept them, and my dad kept them. Now I have them sitting in my office to remind me of this story. During World War II in France, my grandfather Edwin McDonald was a soldier who was shot in the line of duty. He served in France in some of the early days of the war. He didn't last very long; a shell fragment from a German 88 took him out. He was in 18 different hospitals over 3 years before they could figure out how to stitch him back together.

When he got out, there were a lot of things he could not do, but he never complained, and he found a way. Decided that he wanted to start a small restaurant he went to the bank which had no record of him, but they trusted him and believed someone who fought for our country so with just a signature they gave him the money to go and start his restaurant you name the place the Tic Tock.

The Tic Tock restaurant was in the south side of Chicago in the early 1940s and 1950s. He was a tremendously savvy businessman that kept meticulous records of Everything.

179

He spent most mornings going and buying fresh materials ready to ensure that the customers at the Tic Tock restaurant had nothing but the best. He was fair to his employees. He kept detailed records and ensured that no one would ever go hungry. Then came the Great Migration, and he needed to move back to the farm. But the only person who wanted to buy the restaurant was Ms. Davis. As an African American woman in the 1950's, she did not have access to the same resources that my grandfather did. So, they found a compromise. My grandfather would give her the restaurant, which was his life savings. But Ms. Davis had no down payment, no collateral, and no one to sign the loan with her. But she would need to keep up with her payments every month on time. If she missed even one payment, he could cancel the agreement. She never missed a payment.

They didn't keep in touch much other than an occasional Christmas Card. But one day, 20 years later, in the middle of the afternoon, Ms. Davis called up my grandfather and said, "I just wanted to say, Thank you for giving a young, poor black woman a chance." My grandfather responded, "I needed you as much as you needed me."

Farmer vs. Multinational Corporation

In 2015, the Village of Nickerson, Nebraska, was told that a large company would be moving into the area. However, community members weren't told who the company was or what they would be doing. Soon, community members discovered that it was going to be Costco. The proposed project that Costco wanted to develop was the largest poultry processing facility in U.S. history. This was troubling on many levels.

The first concern was that this would harm local agricultural markets. As this would be the first time that a retail giant owned the complete supply chain. This type of vertical integration has taken away the ability of family farmers to compete. In this model Costco can sell their 5$ chickens as what's called a loss leader. They take a loss on the chickens but make up the profit everywhere else. Unfortunately, the family farmers end up just losing their market.

Then there were concerns regarding the effect on local water quality and soil health. The large scale model would spike the nitrates and ammonia levels. This could have significant

183

adverse effects on area water and health. If there were damages Costco setup a shell company named Lincoln Premium Poultry (LPP).

They were also concerned the project head was formerly with Pilgrim's Pride. In that work he had made many promises about the benefits for family farmers and community. Unfortunately, they ended up being not true. Instead family farmers signed contracts with stipulations that were almost impossible to meet. When they couldn't keep up they would basically lose their farms. All the risk was given to the farmer and all the profit was given to the corporation.

This troubled a group of local family farmers. One, in particular, was a quiet farmer with a prominent beard who decided he wanted to take more action. He approached a prominent local attorney to take legal action but was advised that the legal process was stacked against him. He could try to pursue legal action but would be unlikely to succeed. Multinational corporations had been lobbying for decades to allow for operations like these.

So, the attorney referred him to me and my frequent collaborator Graham Christensen. We met Randy at a small local restaurant in West Omaha and talked about the local need. We heard stories of family farms held for generations and his wonderful community. Then how his legitimate concerns about the damage this operation would do.

This began our work organizing to create what eventually became Nebraska Communities United. Grassroots organizing around these concerns stopped the project in Nickerson. Soon after, the neighboring city, Fremont, became the official site of the massive facility. Over 500 production barns would need to be built in the surrounding communities. This would cause permanent damage to those local communities and the farming way of life.

But those grassroots leaders under the banner of Nebraska Communities United kept working. They realized the dangers of extreme vertically integrated operations would keep coming. If they wanted to stop this they needed to start organizing. They started with educational meetings with local farmers about the poultry grower contracts. This helped to spread awareness and provide the farmers with the knowledge of what to watch for.

As more barns sought permits other communities became aware of the dangers. We worked to develop these local communities into an agile organization ready to respond. As we continued to educate and advocate many conversations around these issues started. These conversations about what they didn't want shifted to what they did want. They wanted family farms that produced nutritious food while protecting our land and water. They realized that their soil quality kept going down while their expenses increased.

As new barn proposals popped up all over the state, we fought back barn by barn. This energy led to a battle over the rural communities in Lancaster County. Two more local groups developed in the county. One around the southern hills area and one in the northern area surrounding a small school in Raymond, Nebraska.

As we continued to educate and advocate, we had many conflicts between neighbors and friends. But the tide began to turn. Lancaster County Planning Commission voted for the project. But the interesting part was their justification. They didn't like it but felt limited regulatory standards required project approval. The chair noted they were unprepared for these types of operations. They went on to call for a task force to review these standards.

This turning point was huge. As we worked with the task force and the county board we saw a shift. They continued to hear from concerned the concerned community about the potential dangers. As we provided them reports, experts, and technical guidance they realized what could happen. This led the task force and the county board to recommend some huge improvements. Their were protections for farmers, water, schools, and neighbors. These standards were the best in the state and have continued to grow conversations.

Trinity's Story

I have two sisters. The first, Field, just a year and a half younger than me is incredibly intelligent, well-spoken, and creative. She is traveled around the world, visiting 21 countries. She is currently in Columbia. The video montages she puts together seem to be already professionally done. I am very proud of her.

A few years younger than her, my sister Trinity is kind, enthusiastic, and energetic. She is the student council president, has an album of her music, and has created some of my favorite art pieces. Everyone knows her for her running tackle hugs that could knock over any Husker lineman. I am very proud of her. According to the Nebraska Youth Suicide Prevention site, "Suicide is the 2nd leading cause of death for Nebraska youth ages 15-19." In October 2013, my sister Trinity was one of those affected.

It was traumatic, jarring, and still does not make sense. But it is what happened. It is not something that is pleasant to talk about. Yet, I feel compelled to talk about this issue because it's an issue that is too severe and too large not to talk about. It is not a subject that many even begin to know how to address. Yet, it has thrown blow after devastating blow to our communities.

Particularly we have seen the effects on Lincoln. The school district and community has begun to react with a more holistic approach but there is a long way to go.

We need a more significant focus on mental health at all levels. These are not just issues in Nebraska, nor are they issues limited to a specific demographic. These issue affect people of all ages, racial backgrounds, and economic backgrounds. I have seen these issues plague my friends, my peers, and my community members. Yet, it seems that we are still too timid to approach these with the open, caring compassion that we need. It happens to the smart, the athletic, the talented, the kind, the involved, and any other kind of person you can think of. Mental health issues affect far more people than we even realize.

We often have no idea until it is too late. Which is why we need vigilance, funding for research, training, funding for prevention, acceptance, and understanding of these vital issues. It is hard to wonder if perhaps someone missed something. What if something could have been done? I would do anything to find that possibility. For Trinity, we can't find a solution, but perhaps we can find another step that could save someone else, so maybe their brother can tell them how proud they are."

This is the most powerfully driving story in my life. This continues to drive me and has led to many trainings, the passage of a new suicide prevention bill, new community task forces, and more.

Celeste is a beautiful, happy, and fun-loving three-year-old. She loves books, knocking down block towers, and going to the swimming pool. When you see her, she will most likely have one of her award-winning smiles for you. Her disability doesn't define her, but it is a huge factor in her life. Her diagnoses include: a brain cyst, 5 agenesis of the corpus callosum, hypotonia, aberrant subclavian artery, malrotation, hearing loss, exotropia, oral aversion, and previous failure to thrive but now tube fed. Nearly 100% of her calories are put through the tube. She is also suspected (not yet confirmed) to have a tethered spinal cord. Her family is also currently awaiting approval for further genetic testing because even with the feeding tube she's very petite. All these diagnoses together make it difficult for Celeste to live the life of a typical three-year-old. She doesn't stand on her own, walk, or talk and is nowhere near being ready for potty training. She can't consume enough calories on her own to sustain herself. She can't have normal

194

bowel movements without medications to help her. She is at a higher risk of bowel obstructions or life-threatening volvulus in her intestines. Celeste's family has private insurance, but without a Medicaid waiver, her family would be paying nearly $1,400 a month just for the necessary medical supplies and specialized formulas. This doesn't even include the necessary therapies Celeste requires in order to reach her maximum potential or the childcare necessary for her parents to maintain their teaching careers. Without the waiver, her parents would have to work additional jobs to cover the nearly $2,000 worth of bills; but, that would add additional stress fitting in nearly 40 hours a week on top of teaching and getting Celeste to her therapies--exposure to stress that Celeste doesn't need or deserve. Another option would be for them to quit their careers and move to lower-paying jobs in order to meet the income requirements to qualify for Medicaid, move out of state or take on an astronomical amount of debt. The idea of losing the waiver has led to a great deal of stress and even the consideration of keeping Celeste out of therapy for fear of her making "too much progress." The waiver for Celeste has meant more than medical bills being paid- it's more time with her parents at home helping to extend what she does in therapy. It has meant time for her parents to use respite care and invest in their marriage, son, careers, and community.

When a group of children like Celeste's Medicaid access was cut a group of Families came together to form a coalition calling for us to improve our Medicaid Home and Community Based Waiver System.

Petition Drive

This led to over 1600 petition signatures we gathered at the heart of this campaign. These signers were part of a critical engagement tool, created pressure, and captured press attention. The National Press Coverage amped up the pressure on the administration. Most importantly, this was just step one. The funneled to massively increased engagement, membership sign-ups, donors, and volunteers.

Waiver Study

When diving into our values, we saw that we needed to have multiple levels of the conversation. Most people can only remember a sentence; some can hear a presentation, some will have personal conversations with their Senators. This helped to serve as a base document to center the movement and set a more specific direction. This helped to capture the stories and show how policy relates to stories.

Pathways to Medicaid

We did a series of presentations across the state to educate and arm our members. Most people don't understand the issues involved because they are purposely complicated. We need to do a better job of ensuring that overwhelmed parents can really comprehend and quickly act in a limited time. These in-person conversations also allow for dialogue and community forming. Another helpful tool we have been using more frequently is Facebook Live which allows increased engagement from parents who may not be able to make an event usually.

This coalition work led to improved notice standards, increased funding in the area, increased education, and many families getting back onto services. We are headed to get many more children with disabilities served.

Where Does

It End?

The hardest part of writing this book has undoubtedly been finding an ending. But the truth is this isn't an end. This is just a beginning. What happens next is up to you. How you use these tools and ideas is up to you.

If you are still reading I know you care about stories, prioritize values, and care deeply for your community. We need people like you who care about neighbors, friends, and their broader community. This kind of work is difficult and can take time but is so important.

Remember you can create a better world and create the change you want to see through organizing. If you bring people together around a common goal you can accomplish amazing things. If you keep having those kitchen table conversations, knock on some more doors, and keep sharing ideas you will get there. I hope that this book has provided you some guidance to create the change you want to see. I hope that you get more people healthcare, or protect your water, or even get that new streetlight. Whatever you do I'm sure you will create a better world.

What I've come to realize is that's because there is no end. This is just a seed. I look forward to the seeds you will plant and the change you will harvest.

If you need resources, more helpful information, help looking for a job in organizing, want a certification, a template campaign plan, or other resources, then check out The Political Garage at Elmwayconsulting.com

References

"Robert M. Pirsig Quotes." BrainyQuote.com. BrainyMedia Inc,

2021. 27 October 2021.

https://www.brainyquote.com/quotes/robert_m_pirsig_676382

"Noam Chomsky Quotes." BrainyQuote.com. BrainyMedia Inc,

2021. 27 October 2021.

https://www.brainyquote.com/quotes/noam_chomsky_635769

"Paul Wellstone Quotes." BrainyQuote.com. BrainyMedia Inc,

2021. 27 October 2021.

https://www.brainyquote.com/quotes/paul_wellstone_361494

"Dolores Huerta Quotes." BrainyQuote.com. BrainyMedia Inc,

2021. 27 October 2021.

https://www.brainyquote.com/quotes/dolores_huerta_875573

Out of the Darkness and Into the Light - MN.

https://mn.gov/mnddc/parallels2/pdf/00s/02/02-out-of-the-

darkness.pdf

"Wit & Wisdom." The Week, no. 987, Dennis Publishing Ltd.,

Sept. 2014, p. 23.

Top 10 Nonprofit Email Marketing Tools - ELEVATION.

https://blog.elevationweb.org/nonprofit-email-marketing-tools

8 Awesome Nonprofit CRM Options for Your Organization ....

https://blog.elevationweb.org/6-awesome-nonprofit-crm-

options

NationBuilder Software - 2021 Reviews, Pricing & Demo.

https://www.softwareadvice.com/nonprofit/nationbuilder-

profile/

Gerber, Alan S., and Donald P. Green. "The Effects of
Canvassing, Telephone Calls, and Direct Mail on Voter
Turnout: A Field Experiment." JSTOR. The American Political
Science Review, n.d. Web. 25 Feb. 2014.

Gerber, Alan S., and Donald P. Green. "Does Canvassing
Increase Voter Turnout? A Field Experiment." JSTOR. National
Academy of Sciences, n.d. Web. 02 May 2014.

Parry, Janine, Jay Barth, Martha Kropf, and E. Terrence Jones.
"Mobilizing the Seldom Voter: Campaign Contact and Effects in
High-Profile Elections." JSTOR. Political Behavior, n.d. Web. 02
May 2014.

https://www.linkedin.com/pulse/effectiveness-direct-contact-
vote-mail-efforts-nebraska-edison/

http://cdrnys.org/disability-writing-journalism-guidelines/

http://michaelbrand.org/why-our-service-clubs-are-dying/

About the Author

Edison McDonald is a community-centered professional focused
on transforming communities. He believes that connecting
people with the resources they need is vital to the success of our
society. He has worked in communities, nonprofits, for-profits,
political organizations, faith organizations in Washington D.C.,
Illinois, Iowa, and across Nebraska to help create a better world.
He is continually working to create change, whether by writing
grants to produce more renewable energy, leading campaigns to

bring better leaders, advocating to change laws, or working directly to organize communities.

"The place to improve the world is first in one's own heart and head and hands, and then work outward from there." — Robert M. Pirsig